THE DANES IN AMERICA

THE DANES
IN AMERICA

Peter L. Petersen

Lerner Publication Company · Minneapolis

Front cover: *A photograph to send home. Lewis and Mary Juhl, six of their eight children, and the family pets pose in front of the house on their newly purchased farm near Irwin, Iowa, in 1912. Photos such as these recorded the economic success of once-poor Danish immigrants and were often sent to relatives and friends who remained in Denmark.*
Page 2: *The class of a one-room school in rural Minnesota, 1912. Many of the students are first-generation Americans whose parents emigrated from Denmark and other Scandinavian countries.*

For the next generation: Eric, Brant, Steven, Christopher, Scott, Amy, Cynthia, Julie, Cara

Library of Congress Cataloging-in-Publication Data

Petersen, Peter L., 1935-
    The Danes in America.

    (In America series)
    Includes index.
    Summary: Surveys the Danish immigration to the
United States and discusses the contributions made
by Danes to various areas of American life.
    1. Danish Americans—History—Juvenile literature.
[1. Danish Americans] I. Title. II. Series.
E184.S19P48 1987   973'.043981   86-20877
ISBN 0-8225-0233-X (lib. bdg.)
ISBN 0-8225-1031-6 (pbk.)

1 2 3 4 5 6 7 8 9 10 97 96 95 94 93 92 91 90 89 88 87

CONTENTS

1
THE LAND THEY CAME FROM

This statue of the beloved Danish writer Hans Christian Andersen stands in Copenhagen's Royal Gardens.

The Fourth of July in Denmark

On every Fourth of July since 1912 (excepting the years during the two World Wars), Danes, Danish Americans, and Americans have gathered on the heather-covered hills of Rebild, a small national park south of the Danish city of Aalborg, to celebrate the independence of the United States. Acclaimed as the largest Fourth of July observance held outside the United States, the Rebild Festival annually attracts between 20,000 and 40,000 people. The program features singing, including the national anthems of both nations, and speeches from prominent Danes and Americans, ranging in past years from Danish monarchs to Americans such as Hubert Humphrey and Walt Disney.

Near the center of Rebild National Park stands a log cabin, its walls built of timbers from forests scattered throughout the United States. Like the several hundred acres of land that make up the park, the log cabin was a gift to the Danish nation from Danes who had emigrated to the United States and from their descendants. Nearby are twin flag poles from which fly the Stars and Stripes of the United States and the Danish flag, called *Dannebrog.*

For many citizens of Denmark and the United States, Rebild National Park, its Fourth of July celebrations, and the "Lincoln Log" cabin serve not only as symbols of the long and peaceful relations between the two nations but also as reminders that more than 370,000 Danes emigrated to the United States.

The flags of Denmark and the United States fly over the crowd assembled for the Fourth of July celebration at Rebild National Park.

NORTH SEA

Göteborg

SWEDEN

Alborg
Rebild

JUTLAND

DENMARK

Billund

Helsingør

Copenhagen

Odense

BALTIC
SEA

Kiel

WEST
GERMANY

EAST
GERMANY

The Land and People of Denmark

Denmark is the smallest and southernmost of the Scandinavian nations. It consists of a narrow peninsula called Jutland, an extension of continental Europe pointing north from the Federal Republic of Germany, and 483 islands, 97 of which are inhabited. The total land area is approximately 17,000 square miles, slightly less than half the size of the state of Indiana. In addition, Denmark owns sparsely populated Greenland, the largest island in the world, and the 17 Faroe Islands, located northwest of Scotland.

The country has a population of 5,200,000 people, one-fourth of whom live in the lovely capital city of Copenhagen. The Nordic element, with its characteristically blond, curling hair and blue eyes, is dominant among the Danes, but the region long has been a geographic crossroads and hence the Danish people are of mixed stock. The Danish language belongs to the East Scandinavian group of Germanic languages. Most Danes are members of the Evangelical Lutheran Church.

One unusual fact about the Danish people that visitors often notice is so many of them have similar names. In a large part this is due to the ancient practice called patronymics, by which Jens, the son of Peter, became Jens Petersen, and Jens' son John became John Jensen. Under this system, the surname changed with each generation.

But a government decree in 1856 said that henceforth surnames would not change, and thus Danes became Petersens or Jensens for good.

Today 60 percent of all Danish surnames end in "sen." About half of the population shares 14 names—Jensen (370,000) and Nielsen (350,000) are the most common. This often creates problems. For example, there are 32,000 Jensens listed in the Copenhagen phone book. By comparison, the phone directory for New York's Manhattan, with a slightly larger population, has only 3,100 Smiths, the most common American name.

The Jensens, Nielsens, and Petersens of modern Denmark are inhabitants of a prosperous land with one of the highest standards of living in the world. Today as in the past, agriculture is an important part of the Danish economy.

Danes walking along Strøget, a colorful pedestrian shopping street in Copenhagen. These citizens of modern Denmark enjoy one of the world's highest standards of living.

One of the country's greatest assets, second perhaps only to its people, has been an abundance of fertile land. Almost 75 percent of the land area is devoted to agriculture.

Two developments have allowed Danish farmers to excel: the growth of producer and marketing cooperatives; and a tendency toward product specialization. Danish dairy, poultry, and swine products have high reputations, and about two-thirds of the nation's farm production goes to the export market. Large portions of the catch by Danish fisherman are also exported.

In recent years, much of the growth in the Danish economy has come in its industrial segment. The largest industry is iron and steel, and Danes are world-famous ship builders. By one estimate, Danes supply about 30 percent of the engines that power the world's largest ships. Denmark is also famous for its brewing industry. Carlsberg and Tuborg beers are sold worldwide. A portion of the profits from the sale of these beers goes into a fund that supports artistic and scientific endeavors.

Tourism is another important factor in the modern Danish economy. Every year thousands of foreign visitors flock to Copenhagen to enjoy the city's exciting night life, to stroll through Tivoli, a delightful amusement park that first opened its gates in 1843, and to look for bargains along Strøget, a long pedestrian shopping street. For those who can tear themselves away from Copenhagen's charms, there are many enticements outside the capital.

A performer dressed as Pierrot invites visitors to pass through the gates of Tivoli. This comic character from traditional European pantomime is the symbol of the famous Danish amusement park.

Tourists in Denmark often visit Legoland (right), an entertainment center located in Jutland. Here they can see an amazing collection of miniature scenes constructed completely out of the small plastic components known as Lego. Nearby is the factory that manufactures 400,000 Lego pieces each hour.

Another famous Danish landmark is Krønberg Castle (below), located in the coastal city of Helsingør. This massive castle is the setting of Shakespeare's Hamlet, a play about a legendary Danish prince.

A reconstruction of one of the Viking ships found on the bottom of the sea near the village of Skuldelev. In vessels like these, Danish Vikings set sail in search of plunder and trade.

Denmark and the World

The sea has always played a significant role in Danish history. No Dane lives more than 35 miles from the sea coast, and except for three narrow passages, Jutland and the Danish islands form a barrier between the North Sea and the Baltic. About a thousand years ago, this closeness to the sea, combined with economic necessity and a love of adventure, drove fierce Danes called Vikings into contact with other peoples and other lands.

Viking ships brought Danes and other Northmen to present-day Great Britain, France, Holland, and several countries bordering the Mediterranean. For a brief time, between 1013 and 1042, a Danish king ruled England. Not only did Viking raiding parties return with ships loaded with plunder and trade goods, but they also brought back news of Christianity. Late in the 10th century, King Harald Bluetooth was baptized. (The current Danish Queen, Margrethe II, traces her office to Harald's father, Gorm the Old, while Sweyn Folkbeard, Harald's son, was the conqueror of England and Norway.)

Soon the forces of King and Church were welding the Danes into a united nation, thus making Denmark one of the oldest kingdoms in the world. For a time, Denmark was a great power of northern Europe, controlling Norway, southern Sweden, and a portion of northern Germany. During the 1600s and 1700s, however, the emergence of powerful rivals, especially Sweden and Germany, and a series of disastrous wars reduced Denmark's size and power.

Left: King Canute (right), the son of the conqueror Sweyn Folkbeard, ruled England from 1013 to 1042.

Below: The present royal family of Denmark is descended from the same ancient line. This photograph, taken in 1966, shows Princess (now Queen) Margrethe (fourth from right) with her future husband and his family (on the left side of the balcony), her parents, King Frederik and Queen Ingrid, and her sister Princess Benedikte (right).

2
EARLY DANISH CONTACT WITH NORTH AMERICA

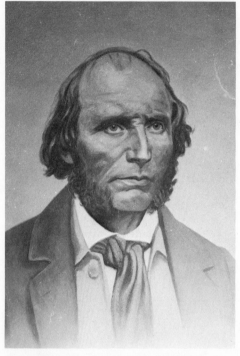

Peter Lassen, a Danish immigrant who was a pioneer in the American West

Explorers and Planters

Scholars still debate who was the first Dane to set foot on North American soil. Some believe that Erik Upsi (or Gnupson), a bishop in Greenland, may have visited North America in the year 1121. Others think that the honor should go to a navigator named Johannes Skolp, who reportedly reached American shores in 1475, 17 years before Christopher Columbus. It is certain, however, that a Danish explorer named Jens Munk reached North America in 1619, only 12 years after the establishment of the English settlement at Jamestown.

Christian IV, the king of Denmark, had commissioned Munk to find the Northwest Passage to the fabulous riches of the Orient. The explorer, with two ships and 65 men, sailed past the southern tip of Greenland, then through

Hudson Strait into Hudson Bay. Unable to find a water route to the West, Munk turned to the southwest and decided to winter near the mouth of what is now called the Churchill River.

The first few weeks went reasonably well, and the expedition, led by its chaplain, Rasmus Jensen, celebrated Christmas in the traditional Danish manner—the first Lutheran Christmas service in North America. After Christmas, however, severe weather and illness began to take their toll among the explorers. By April more than half were dead; by June only Munk and two others remained alive. As the weather became warmer, the three survivors were able to make the smaller of their two ships seaworthy. They valiantly set sail for home, arriving safely on

This woodcut from Jens Munk's published account of his voyage pictures the explorer's two ships, the Unicorn *and the* Lamprey, *and some scenes from his expedition. On the lower left, several of Munk's men are shown shooting a reindeer. In the scene above, the Danes meet some of the inhabitants of the Hudson Bay region, who, despite the cold climate, are pictured naked.*

An early Danish sugar-cane mill on the Caribbean island of St. Croix

Christmas Day in 1620.

Despite the loss of life, Christian IV ordered Munk to retrace his journey and plant a Danish colony in the New World. But ill health prevented the sea captain from carrying out the instructions of his king. Thus Denmark missed an opportunity to become one of the earliest European colonizers of North America.

About a century after Munk's ill-fated expedition, another Danish explorer, Vitus Jonassen Bering, sailing under a Russian flag, determined in 1728 that the Asian and North American continents were divided by water. (The body of water was later named the Bering Sea in his honor.) Thirteen years later, on another expedition, Bering discovered Alaska and several of the Aleutian Islands.

Although Denmark failed to establish a colony on the continent of North America, Danes did settle on the islands of the Caribbean. In 1666, the Danish West Indies Company took possession of the island of St. Thomas. When the agricultural productivity of St. Thomas declined, settlers migrated to nearby St. John, which came under Danish control in 1717. Then in 1733 Denmark purchased St. Croix from France.

In fields worked by slaves imported from Africa, Danish planters in the Caribbean raised tobacco, cotton, and sugar, and carried on extensive commerce first with the English colonies and then later the United States. In the 19th century, however, the plantations became less successful due to the abolition of slavery in 1848 and the decline in the price of raw sugar because of increased production of beet sugar in Europe. The Danish West Indies became an economic liability, and in 1917, Denmark sold the islands to the United States for $25 million. Today known as the Virgin Islands, they hold the status of U. S. territories.

The First Danish Americans

Individual Danes were numbered among the earliest groups of North American settlers, particularly the Dutch in New Netherlands (later New York). That Danes should be mixed in with the Dutch is not surprising since the two nations had much in common during the 17th century. Both were seafaring countries, and this, combined with their geographic closeness, meant sizable trade among their respective citizens. Dutch merchants lived in Denmark, while Danish tradesmen and sailors lived in the Netherlands.

By 1642, approximately 50 of the 1,000 people living in the Dutch colony of New Netherlands were Danes. The first Danish family to emigrate to the colony were the Jansens—Jan, his wife, Engelje, and their four children. The Jansen family came in 1636 and eventually adopted the Dutch name of Van Breestede.

Three years later, two other Danes, Jonas Bronck and Jochem Pietersen Kuyter, arrived. Kuyter was the first settler in that part of New York City known today as Harlem. Bronck, for whom the modern borough of the Bronx is named, purchased 500 acres of land from the Indians for two rifles, two kettles, two overcoats, two shirts, two axes, a barrel of apple cider, and six gold coins. The son of a Danish pastor, Bronck was an educated man, and his large stone house, well-stocked with books shipped from Europe, became the cultural center of the new city.

Another Dane among the Dutch, Jacob Steendam, was the colony's first poet, while Harry Albertsen made the first bricks. By 1664, when the English captured New Amsterdam and changed its name to New York, the Danes were already beginning to scatter, with some living in New Jersey and others in the city of Albany. After the Dutch loss of New Amsterdam, Danish emigration declined.

The next group of Danes to move to America were members of a religious group called the Moravian Brethren. Along with emphasizing pious religious observances, the Moravians believed in a form of community living. Adherence to this belief was against Danish law, so many Danish converts decided to emi-

In the mid-1600s, New Amsterdam (later New York) was a small village on the southern tip of Manhattan Island. About 50 of its 1,000 inhabitants were Danes.

grate to a newly formed Moravian settlement at Bethlehem, Pennsylvania. The first to arrive was Christian Werner in 1742. He was soon followed by several others who sailed on ships provided by the Brethren. But the vast majority of Moravians who settled in Bethlehem were German, and therefore the Danes soon blended into the dominant German culture.

With the exception of those who settled among the Dutch and the German Moravians, almost all of the Danes who emigrated to the New World before 1850 came as isolated individuals. Most scattered throughout the vast land, apparently living very ordinary lives and soon losing their ethnic identity. A handful of these early Danes, however, deserves mention.

Hans Christian Febiger (sometimes Fibiger) was one of George Washington's most trusted officers during the American Revolution. Born on the island of Funen in 1746, he received a military education before sailing to the Danish West Indies, where his uncle was a government official. In 1772 Febiger came to the American colonies and settled in Boston. Soon he was engaged in a lively trade of lumber, horses, and fish along the coast from Maine to North Carolina.

Febiger joined a local militia shortly after the first battle of the war was fought at Lexington on April 19, 1775. Because of his military training, he assumed a position of leadership and was rapidly promoted. By 1777 he had risen to the rank of colonel. Febiger, who was fondly called "Old Denmark" by the men under his command, fought in major battles at Bunker Hill, Brandywine, Monmouth, and Yorktown. At the end of the war, he retired from the military with the rank of brigadier general, which had been bestowed upon him by a grateful Congress. Eventually he moved to Philadelphia and married Elizabeth Carson, daughter of a local merchant. In 1789 he was elected Treasurer of Pennsylvania and held that office until his death in 1796 at age 50.

Christian Guldager (or Gallager) was another Dane with ties to George Washington and the War for American Independence. Born in 1759, Guldager was only 17 when his paintings won him the Gold Medal of the Academy of Fine Arts in Copenhagen. As part of the prize, Guldager was given the privilege of studying abroad for three years at government expense. Instead of following the traditional path to Italy, Guldager responded to an invitation from Ben Franklin and came to America.

Guldager's choice was a good one, and he soon won fame and fortune as a portrait artist. His portrait of Washington is widely considered to be one of the best of the American hero. For many years, it was believed that Guldager was also the designer of the defiant eagle that adorns the Great Seal of the United States. Recent research, however, has failed to discover any ties between the Danish artist and the American symbol.

Still another Danish painter found a different revolutionary war—this one to gain Texas independence. Charles Zan-

Christian Guldager's portrait of George Washington

co emigrated to Texas in 1834, just in time to be swept up in the struggle against Mexico. Shortly after joining a local resistance group, Zanco was called upon to paint a white star on a banner of blue silk. Below the "lone star" was the word "Independence." Ultimately, however, Zanco made a far greater contribution to the cause of Texas independence. Five months later, in March 1836, he died defending the Alamo. As a reminder of Zanco's sacrifice, a Danish flag stands today in one corner of the Alamo Chapel.

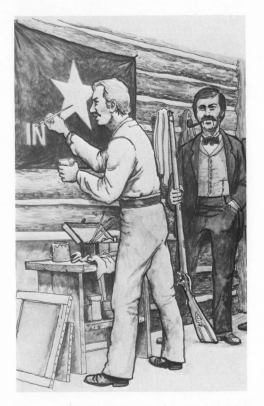

While Charles Zanco was fighting and dying for Texas independence, Peter Lassen was in Missouri preparing to help push the American frontier westward. Lassen was born in Denmark in 1800. His father was Lars Nielsen, and so Peter took the last name of Larsen. But over the years it changed from Larsen to Larssen to Lassen, with the final name going down in history.

Lassen was a blacksmith and followed that trade for a time after his arrival in the United States in 1830. He settled briefly in Keytesville, Missouri, about 100 miles east of Kansas City. When the opportunity arose, he joined with a

Five months after Charles Zanco painted the "lone star" on the Texas flag (left), the Danish artist died in the battle of the Alamo (below).

California's Mount Lassen was named after a Danish immigrant who played an important role in the early history of the state.

group of adventurers heading west and thus helped blaze the trail followed by the "forty-niners." After first going to Oregon, Lassen sailed down the coast to California. He continued to work as a blacksmith, but also built the first sawmill in California in order to supply lumber for the towns springing up around the gold fields and along the coast.

One day, while chasing horse thieves in the north, he found near Deer Creek a beautiful area of land that greatly appealed to him. In 1844 he staked a claim to 22,000 acres and began to dream of founding a colony or city on his new holdings. But his dream did not come true. After suffering financial setbacks in ranching and gold prospecting, Lassen was forced to sell his Deer Creek lands. He moved to the Honey Lake and Susanville area and, in 1859, was killed, apparently by Indians. Considered one of the pioneers of California, Lassen has been honored in several ways. An inactive volcano in northern California, a California county, and a national park all bear his name.

By the time of Peter Lassen's death, events were already underway in both Denmark and the United States that would bring more than 350,000 additional Danes to America. A great migration was about to begin.

3

THE GREAT MIGRATION

A poster of a steamship line invites Danish emigrants to travel to America.

Why They Came

According to statistics collected by the United States Immigration Service, 371,258 immigrants arrived from Denmark between 1820, when the government first began to count arrivals, and 1980. The great majority—242,544—came between 1850 and 1930. The peak year was 1882, when 11,618 Danes emigrated to America. Although these figures may appear small when compared with the number of migrants from countries such as Ireland, Italy, or Germany, they represent a significant loss of population for tiny Denmark—approximately 1 out of every 10 ten of its citizens.

Why did so many Danes emigrate to the United States? The answer to that question is more complicated than it first appears. A sizable migration of people from any country usually involves many factors, perhaps several for each person who made the journey. Generally, however, it is recognized that migration is the result of a complicated combination of both "push" and "pull" factors. This means that there were things happening in Denmark that pushed people into the emigrant stream at the same time that conditions in the United States were pulling them across the Atlantic.

Often these push and pull factors are so intertwined that it is impossible to separate them. Nevertheless, recent studies made in both the United States and Denmark have revealed an abundance of reasons for immigration, most of which fit into either the push or pull category.

To America for Religious Reasons
The Baptists

Clearly religion was a motivating factor for some Danish emigrants. Toward the middle of the 19th century, certain religious movements started to gain converts in Denmark despite the opposition of the Lutheran State Church. Baptists began appearing in 1839 when a Dane named Julius Købner returned to Copenhagen from Hamburg, Germany, where he had been converted. He was soon joined by the man who had baptized him, J. G. Oncken, and the two began to teach, preach, and baptize.

The Danish government frowned upon such activity and persecuted many Baptist converts by fining and imprisoning them. Rather than try to practice their faith in such a hostile atmosphere, some Baptists chose to emigrate. It is probable that one out of every three of these early converts left Denmark, often traveling in groups. In 1854, nine members from the Vanløse church near Copenhagen established in Potter County, Pennsylvania, the first Danish Baptist congregation in the United States. There can be little doubt that the promise of religious freedom influenced their decision to come to America.

The Potter County church lasted only a few years. Most of its founders soon moved west and settled in Wisconsin, where they were joined by other Baptists migrating directly from Denmark. Eventually, several members of the Wisconsin congregations moved on to Minnesota and Iowa, taking their faith with them. The total number of Danish Baptists who emigrated is impossible to determine. One scholar estimates that in 1909, there were probably no more than 5,000 in the United States, and that figure includes some children and grandchildren born in America.

Why such a small number? One reason was the slow but steady growth of religious toleration in Denmark. A new constitution was adopted in 1849, and even though it maintained the established church, it allowed the formation of non-Lutheran denominations. Although persecution did not cease immediately, Baptists gradually came to believe that they no longer had to leave Denmark to practice their faith.

A second reason for the small number of Baptist immigrants was the success of missionaries from the Church of Jesus Christ of Latter-day Saints, or Mormons, in winning converts among the members of Baptist congregations in Denmark. Many of these people migrated, but they came to the United States as Mormons, not as Baptists.

The Mormons

Mormon converts migrating to Utah represent the first large wave of Danish emigration to the United States. In the 20-year period between 1850 and 1870, 16,760 Danes emigrated to America. Of that number, 7,480 (45 percent) were Mormons. By 1904, the year that Mormons in Denmark stopped recruiting emigrants, 12,260 Danes had made the difficult and often dangerous pilgrimage to the Mormon "Zion" in the valley of Utah's Great Salt Lake. Mormon missionaries were more successful in Denmark than in any other European country except England.

There are several explanations for Mormon success in Denmark. For one thing, the first Mormon missionaries arrived in 1850, just a year after the adoption of the constitution that granted the right to worship to any faith as long as it did not conflict with public decency. Another advantage enjoyed by the missionaries was the close relationship between Mormon leader Brigham Young

Mormon leader Brigham Young was a close friend of the Hansen brothers, two Danes who were early converts to the Mormon faith.

and two Danish brothers, Peter O. and Hans Christian Hansen, who had been converted to the faith in the United States. (Peter O. Hansen's translation of the *Book of Mormon* was the first appearance of that important work in a foreign language.) The ties between Young and the Hansens may explain why, of the first seven Mormon missionaries sent to Europe, three, including Peter O. Hansen, ended up in Denmark.

Finally, Mormons found considerable success in making converts among the ranks of Danish Baptists, who had already been won away from the Lutheran State Church. The first Mormon congregation in Copenhagen was overwhelmingly composed of former

This painting by a Danish Mormon artist, Carl Christian Anton Christensen, pictures the difficult overland journey to Salt Lake City. Like the travelers shown here, many Mormons made the trek on foot, carrying their possessions in hand-carts.

Baptists. Encouraged by their progress in the capital, Mormon missionaries soon began spreading their message among Baptists throughout Denmark, often with favorable results.

Most Mormon converts in Denmark were extremely poor and lacked the financial resources to make the trip to Utah. To ease this problem, a Perpetual Emigration Fund was set up in Salt Lake City in 1850. The fund provided credit to emigrants wishing to make the journey, though the converts had to agree to pay the fund back once they were successfully established in Utah.

Normally Mormon emigrants traveled in groups guided by Mormon leaders, frequently on ships chartered by the church. In the period before the appearance of steamships and the completion of the American trans-continental railroad, the journey from Denmark to Utah frequently required more than six months of difficult travel.

To America for Political Reasons

In 1866, a conservative government "revised" the Danish constitution of 1849 and, in the process, set off a political struggle that went on for the remainder of the century. For some Danes, emigration offered an escape from a seemingly hopeless political situation.

One Dane who supported emigration for political reasons was the fiery radical Mogens Abraham Sommer. Sommer was the spokesman for a blend of social criticism and religion that frequently attracted the interest of those dissatisfied with both state and church in Denmark. In the years between 1867 and 1872, he passionately and repeatedly called upon his countrymen to emigrate, and he personally led several groups of Danes to America. By one count he crossed the Atlantic 13 times.

It is difficult to determine how many people emigrated because of Mogens Sommer's campaign, but one writer observed in 1901, at the time of Sommer's death, that the number of Danes "whom he, directly or indirectly, sent overseas must be counted by the tens of thousands."

Socialists

Danish socialists were among those who felt the hand of government repression in the late 19th century. Sev-

Louis Pio

eral socialist leaders were charged with crimes against public order and authority and sentenced to varying terms in prison. Following their release, two of them, Louis Pio and Poul Geleff, began investigating the possibility of establishing a socialist colony in the United States. Geleff went to Kansas in the summer of 1876 to explore options and conditions there. After his return, he and Pio began to praise the virtues of the colonization scheme and invited dissatisfied Danish socialists to join them in emigrating.

In late March 1877, Pio and Geleff left for the United States. But it was soon revealed that Copenhagen police had

Poul Geleff

Although lacking experience in farming, the men began to prepare the land for planting. But within six weeks, endless wrangling about the true nature of socialism brought the experiment to a humiliating end. The commonly held property was sold, and the proceeds divided among the colonists, who each received about 30 dollars. And thus ended the effort to established a refuge on the prairies of Kansas for Danish socialists.

Even though the socialist colony in Kansas planned by Pio and Geleff failed to materialize, some Danish socialists came to the United States on their own. For years Chicago was the center of Danish-American socialism, but even there the numbers appear small. Most Danes who emigrated to America came to participate in the capitalist system, not to overturn it.

paid the two men a sizable sum of money to leave the country. Upon their arrival in New York, Pio and Geleff had a bitter argument over the division of the funds, and they parted company. Geleff abandoned the colonization project and went to Chicago, where he wrote a pamphlet exposing the arrangement between himself, Pio, and the Danish police.

Undiscouraged by this disclosure, Pio and 18 of his followers went on to Kansas and established their colony on the Smokey Hill River near Hays. They erected a crude log cabin as a common residence, with families living on one side and unmarried men on the other.

Slesvigers

By far the largest number of Danes who came to America for political reasons came from the area of Jutland called North Slesvig. In 1864, following decades of dispute and intrigue, the nation of Prussia defeated Denmark in a short but bitter war. As one consequence of a harsh treaty forced upon the loser, Denmark had to give up North Slesvig and its inhabitants, some 150,000 people who were thoroughly Danish in language and loyalty.

The Prussian occupation of North Slesvig was a bitter one that stressed a

– – – – – –	Southern boundary before 1864
• • • • • • • •	Southern boundary, 1864-1920
• — • — • —	Southern boundary today

Denmark lost North Slesvig to Germany after being defeated in a bitter war.

relentless policy of "Prussianizing" or "Germanizing" the Danish population. (After 1871, when the Prussian king was proclaimed emperor of Germany, the history of Prussia is essentially that of Germany.) The result was a flight of many from this 'lost land' to escape the threat to their way of life and the hated military draft into the German army. This author's paternal grandfather was among those who left.

The Germans put few restrictions on the emigration of Danes from North Slesvig since their departure weakened Danish nationalism in the area while providing more room for an imported German population. German authorities did not keep public records on who left, and the United States listed Danes from North Slesvig as having emigrated from Germany. Therefore, it is difficult to tell how many of these people came to America. But studies of the population after North Slesvig was returned to Denmark in 1920 (the result of a referendum following the German defeat in World War I) suggest that perhaps 50,000 left the territory between 1864 and 1920, the majority going to the United States.

Because of the unusual circumstances, the actual number of Danish immigrants during this period may be significantly higher than the official records indicate. There can be little doubt that a sizable majority of Danish immigrants in the 1850s and 1860s were either Mormons or Slesvigers, people coming to America for essentially religious or political reasons.

Toste Peter Petersen (left) emigrated to the United States from North Slesvig in 1881 to escape service in the German army. In 1896, he married Martha Rasmussen (right), the American-born daughter of immigrants from his home village of Lintrup. In this 1912 photograph, the Petersens and their children are shown standing on the porch of their farm home in Shelby County, Iowa.

To America for Economic Reasons

Following the end of the American Civil War in 1865, Danish emigration to the United States changed from a trickle into a flood. Clearly push and pull factors other than religion and politics were beginning to affect the Danish people.

In common with much of Europe, Denmark was undergoing a population explosion during these years. Improvements in nutrition and medical care had resulted in a sharp decline in deaths among children, and European populations began to soar. Denmark's rose from approximately 900,000 in 1800 to 1,600,000 in 1860 to over 2,500,000 by the beginning of World War I in 1914.

29

During the second half of the 19th century, farms such as the one shown here were in short supply in Denmark, and many children of farm families faced a landless future.

This increase in population had a significant effect on the lives of many Danes. Because the supply of land was quite limited, an increasing number of farm children, particularly those who were not first-born sons, faced a landless future. The surplus rural population, morever, had lowered wages to the point that by 1870 a farmhand's annual income was less than half the estimated expenses of an average household. Under these conditions, many young people could not afford to get married and start their own home. By the mid-1800s, the average age at marriage was 32 years for men and 29 for women.

The Danish historian Kristian Hvidt has used a computer to create a profile of approximately 172,000 Danes, about 90 percent of the total number who departed their homeland between 1868 and 1900. The picture that emerges from Hvidt's studies is one of a restless, often dissatisfied population. In much of rural Denmark, improvements in education and transportation had produced a growing realization that there were possibilities of a better life outside the village or the circumstances of one's birth. This ambition for a better life was soon being expressed in increased migrations, both internal and external.

Many Danes whose unsatisfied ambitions had caused them to leave home traveled only to the nearest provincial town. Here the growth of industry was creating a demand for workers. The availability of these jobs reduced the number of Danes who eventually emigrated to find opportunities. Because industrialism came relatively early to Denmark and its towns and cities were less scattered than those of Norway and Sweden, Danish emigration was both smaller and later than that of its two neighbors.

Even in Danish towns, however, industrial expansion was frequently unable to absorb all the newcomers, and the unemployment rate often hovered between 40 and 50 percent, even in the summer. Some found jobs in the rapidly growing larger cities such as Copenhagen, Aarhus, and Aalborg, but for many migrants, economic conditions in the urban centers were little better than those they had left behind. Reluctantly, then, numerous Danes came to believe that emigration was their only option.

Why did 9 out of every 10 Danes who left their homeland come to the United States? Many things pulled them to American shores, but the major factor was economic opportunity. That the United States was early viewed as a land offering a better life can be seen in a delightful poem for children, *The Flight to America,* written by Christian Winther in 1844. The poem told of two little boys who had decided to run away to America:

You get a country estate as a gift
And money in addition.

They shoe the horses with silver
And stud the wagonwheels, too.
To take the gold at your feet
You only have to bend.

...it hails and snows candy
and rains lemonade.

And there's freedom besides
From morning to night.
You can spit on the floor if you like
And let your cigars burn too.

Hans Christian Andersen also wrote of the wondrous land across the sea. "A pity, then, that America must be so far away," runs the refrain in one of his songs.

But far more important than poems and songs were the efforts of emigration agents, the propaganda spread by steamship companies and American railroads, and the activities of boards of immigration in various Midwestern and Western states. Just as effective was the appeal of the so-called "American Letters" written by Danes in the United States to friends and relatives at home, describing conditions in the "New World." Writing from the Michigan frontier in the 1850s, Christian Jensen reported:

Here is limitless forest land which can be bought for next to nothing. The Americans are honest people. The country is ruled by a president elected for four years. There are good civil courts and many pretty girls. I am going to marry one.

This Danish advertisement for a steamship company gives information about vessels going to the United States, Australia, and other distant lands.

Equally glowing descriptions of the opportunities to be found in the United States came from the pen of Laurits Jacob Fribert, who wrote the first Danish book about emigration to the United States. Published in 1847, his *Haandbog for Emigranter til Amerikas Vest* (*Handbook for Emigrants to the American West*) described the Upper Midwest as the best place for Scandinavians to find inexpensive land.

Rasmus Sørensen also praised the region. After traveling from Copenhagen to Wisconsin in 1852, he wrote a 70-page book describing his experiences. In this and future works, Sørensen stressed that, with hard work, Danish emigrants to Wisconsin could escape the grinding poverty that plagued much of Denmark. Three times before his death in 1865, Sørensen escorted sizable groups of emigrants to North America.

Danish artist Edvard Petersen pictures emigrants on Copenhagen's Larsen Plads quay preparing for departure to the United States. More than 200,000 Danes made the long journey during the years between 1850 and 1930.

33

4
DANISH SETTLEMENTS IN AMERICA

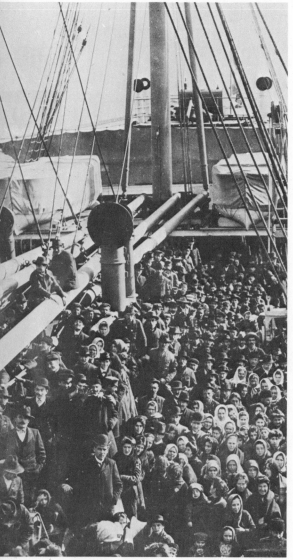

Immigrants crossing the Atlantic in the early 1900s

Rich Farming Lands for All

By 1860 there was evidence that efforts such as those of Fribert and Sørensen were having an impact. In that year, the Danish-born population of Wisconsin rose to 1,150. The first farming settlement had been founded near Hartland in 1845. There soon followed others at New Denmark (later just Denmark) and Neenah. Other Danes settled among the Norwegians in Dane County (named after Nathan Dane of Massachusetts and Revolutionary War fame). Eventually, as the Wisconsin frontier pushed westward, several Danish communities developed near the Minnesota border, including West Denmark in Polk County.

With the end of the war between Prussia and Denmark in 1864 and the American Civil War a year later, Danish emigration began to gather renewed momentum. Of great interest to many Danes was news of the Homestead Act passed in 1862. For land-hungry farm hands, the report that the United States was offering 160 acres free to anyone who asked was almost beyond belief. No country could afford to be that generous with something as precious as land, they insisted.

But it was true, and what was called "American Fever" began to infect parts of Denmark. Rather than remain at home with little hope of ever acquiring land of their own, thousands of poor but ambitious Danes decided to take advantage of the generous land policies of the United States and become farmers in the Midwestern and Great Plains states. As a result, a so-called "Danish belt" of settlement developed in this area between 1860 and 1900, spreading from Wisconsin across northern Illinois and on into Iowa, Minnesota, Nebraska, and South Dakota.

By 1890 Iowa had replaced Wisconsin as the state with the largest Danish-born population. Some of the first Danes who settled in Iowa came from Wisconsin. In 1853, for example, Claus L. Clausen, a Danish-born Lutheran minister, led 40 Danish and Norwegian families, their possessions in ox-drawn wagons, to a colony in Iowa just south of the Minnesota border called St. Ansgar (after a monk credited with bringing Christianity to Denmark). Most of

Claus L. Clausen, a Lutheran minister, established an early Danish-Norwegian colony in Iowa.

Iowa's Danes, however, came directly from Denmark, largely from Jutland.

There were at least three major areas of Danish settlement in Iowa. The earliest was in the vicinity of Cedar Falls and the nearby community of Fredsville (*fred* is the Danish word for peace). Most of the settlers here were Slesvigers who had fled German occupation of their homeland. Further west, in Emmet, Clay, and Palo Alto counties, Danes settled around the communities of Ringsted (named after a town in Denmark) and Graettinger.

The largest concentration of Danes in Iowa, indeed the largest rural settlement of Danes in the United States, was in a 1,000-square-mile area of fertile farmland in Audubon, Cass, Pottawattamie, and Shelby counties. By 1910 these four counties had a combined population of 10,874 people who either had been born in Denmark or were the children of parents born there. At the center of this area was the town of Elk Horn, where Danish was spoken until well after the end of World War I. Danish could also be heard on the streets of nearby Audubon, Harlan, Jacksonville, and Kimballton as late as the 1940s.

This 1911 plat map showing land holdings in a portion of Iowa's Shelby County includes the names of many Danish farmers who settled in the area around the turn of the century.

Jens Nelson (second from left) emigrated from Denmark in 1872. In 1901, he and his wife, Sena (second from right), also Danish-born, settled in Tyler, Minnesota, where Jens, a carpenter, built a house for his family. In this 1895 photograph, the Nelsons are shown with 7 of the 11 children born to them.

In Minnesota, Danish farmers also concentrated in three areas. The initial settlement was in Freeborn County, just north of the Iowa border. Most of the settlers here were Baptists, and the Clarks Grove Community had the largest Danish Baptist congregation in the United States. To the west, the town of Tyler in Lincoln County became the second Danish rural community in Minnesota.

The settlement at Tyler was part of an experiment by the Danish Evangelical Lutheran Church, the earliest and for a time the largest Danish religious organization in the United States. At its annual convention in 1884, members of the Danish Church appointed a committee to locate a parcel of land where Danes could settle in a colony. Eventually the committee decided to purchase a tract of 35,000 acres in Lincoln County from a railroad. The land was first offered to prospective settlers in 1885 at a price of seven dollars an acre. Sales were brisk. The Tyler settlement prospered, and by 1900 there were 1,000 Danes in the county.

In 1908, Askov (earlier known as Partridge) was a small settlement full of tree stumps left over from lumbering operations in this forested area of Minnesota.

The third sizable Danish settlement in Minnesota was named Askov after a famous folk school in Denmark. Begun in 1906, Askov was sponsored by an organization called the *Dansk Folkesamfund* (Danish Folk Society) with the goal of preserving Danish culture in America. Most of the approximately 1,000 Askov settlers came from within the United States and not directly from Denmark.

Askov was located in a heavily wooded part of Minnesota between the Twin Cities and Duluth. The timber around the settlement had either been harvested or had burned in a massive forest fire. Although the land was cheap, settlers had to clear it of massive tree stumps. After some early success in raising potatoes, they turned to growing rutabagas. Today Askov bills itself as "The Rutabaga Capital of the World."

The other state that attracted a significant number of Danish farmers was Nebraska. Danes settled in two major areas of the Cornhusker State, along the Missouri River in Dodge, Douglass, and Washington counties, and in the south central counties of Hamilton, Howard, Kearney, and Nuckolls. Danish names such as Dannebrog (the Danish flag), Dannevirke (an ancient wall across part of south Jutland built to keep out invaders), Kronberg, and Nysted mark some of the Danish settlements in Nebraska.

In 1860 there were less than 3,000 Danes in the states of Wisconsin, Illinois, Iowa, Minnesota, and Nebraska. Forty years later, their numbers had risen to over 77,000. In addition, there were smaller but significant settlements of Danes in South Dakota, Kansas, and Michigan. Even so, Danes tended to be scattered more widely than almost any other ethnic group in the United States.

In 1879, the Sorensen family—Mikkel, Mette, and their 10 children—immigrated to Platte County, Nebraska, where they made a home in a dugout cut into the side of a hill. Later the Sorensens built a house out of the thick sod of the Nebraska prairie and finally moved into a sturdy frame house on their own prosperous farm. This family photograph was taken in the late 1800s.

The flags of Denmark and the United States fly in front of the Ansgar Lutheran Church in Danevang, Texas, 1908.

The Danes Go West

As the Midwestern states filled up and the price of land began to rise sharply after 1900, many Danish Americans undertook a second migration and moved further west, where they were frequently joined by Danes arriving directly from Denmark. Some went to North Dakota (the communities of Bowbells, Daneville, Flaxton, Kenmare, and Norman), Montana (in and around Dagmar near the North Dakota line), or Texas (Danevang near the Gulf Coast). Other migrated across the Canadian border into Alberta. By one count, half of the 21,124 Danes in Canada by 1921 had come from the United States.

After 1920, California replaced Iowa as the state with the most Danish-born residents. Several Danish agriculturists became leaders in specialized areas of food production in the state. At Petaluma, in Sonoma County near San Francisco, Danes helped make that region the center for California poultry and egg production. Around Fresno in the San Joaquin Valley, they were actively involved in raising and marketing fruit, particularly raisins. To the north, in Humbolt County, Danish dairy farmers found the region's moist coastal climate to their liking.

The most recent and certainly the most famous Danish settlement in California is Solvang near Santa Barbara. The name *Solvang* means "sunny field" or "vale" and reflects the pleasant climate of the Santa Ynez Valley, where the town is located. Founded in 1911 as a ranching and dairy-farming community by its sponsor, the Danish Folk Society, Solvang has prospered in recent years as a tourist attraction. More than 2 million visitors annually, many from Los Angeles some 130 miles to the south, come to eat and shop in the town's Danish-style restaurants and stores. The mountain ranch of President Ronald Reagan and his wife, Nancy, is close by, and during elections the Reagans cast their ballots in Solvang.

Other Danish farmers, many of them from the American Midwest, sought land in Washington and Oregon. At Enumclaw, Washington, a settlement begun in the 1880s, they grew vegetables and fruit while raising livestock on relatively small holdings. The Danish community near Junction City, Oregon, did not begin until 1902, when A. C. Nielsen purchased a 1,600-acre ranch and began selling tracts of 10 to 60 acres to fellow Danes.

Founded in 1911 by the Danish Folk Society, today the California town of Solvang is a popular tourist center.

41

Danes in an Urban Setting

Although a majority of Danish emigrants to the United States before 1900 were land-seekers, a significant number found work in American cities. The largest concentration of Danes was in Chicago, where more than 10,000 people born in Denmark lived by the turn of the century. Other urban centers with sizable Danish populations by 1900 were New York, with 5,621; Omaha, Nebraska, and its neighbor, Council Bluffs, Iowa, 3,539; Racine, Wisconsin, 2,815; the Twin Cities of Saint Paul and Minneapolis, 2,679; and San Francisco, 2,171.

Even though there were three distinct Danish neighborhoods in Chicago by 1900, urban Danes usually did not settle in one specific area as many ethnic groups did. Thus it is difficult to identify a historic Danish neighborhood in a city like Omaha or San Francisco. Because Danes seldom received unfriendly receptions when they moved into a non-Danish part of town, they tended to scatter across the city.

Adding to their lack of cohesiveness was the vast occupational differences of these newcomers. A recent study by Philip Friedman of the occupations of Chicago Danes in 1900 found approximately 43 percent of them working in manufacturing, 26 percent in domestic service, and 28 percent in commerce and the professions. Obviously a successful businessman or professional had little in common with a servant or an industrial laborer and frequently chose to live apart from them.

Only rarely were urban Danes identified with a specific occupation. In Racine, Wisconsin, which for several decades had a higher proportion of Danes than any other American city, many Danes worked for the J. I. Case Company, a farm-equipment manufacturer. In Perth Amboy, New Jersey, just outside of New York City, several hundred Danes found work at the New Jersey Terra Cotta Company, a large business owned by two Danes, Eckardt V. Ebbesen and Karl Mathiasen.

World War I and the establishment of restrictive immigration quotas by the United States Congress in the 1920s, combined with economic and political reforms in Denmark, brought a virtual halt to the great migration of Danes to America. Although Danish emigration to the United States never reached the size of that from its neighbors of Norway and Sweden, in little more than 50 years, approximately 1 out of every 10 Danes had packed their often meager belongings and crossed the Atlantic to begin a new life in America. The impact of that migration is still being felt in both countries.

Right: *During the 1800s, this thatched-roof cottage, which still stands in the Danish village of Martofte, was the home of the Christensen family. Below: After the Christensens migrated to America, this farmhouse in Jackson County, Minnesota, became their home. Built in 1904, it has sheltered four generations of the family, whose name was changed to Hansen in the United States.*

5
DANISH-AMERICAN INSTITUTIONS

This authentic 19th-century Danish wind-mill stands in the town of Elk Horn, Iowa.

By 1900, Danish Americans were among the most widely scattered of all the ethnic groups in the United States. The census of that year reported Danes living in every county of California, Connecticut, Idaho, Iowa, Maine, Montana, Nevada, New Jersey, South Dakota, Utah, and Wyoming. There were people of Danish ancestry in all but one county of Massachusetts, Minnesota, Nebraska, New York, North Dakota, Oregon, and Washington.

Despite their scattered settlement and relatively small numbers, Danes were able to develop and maintain for varying lengths of time many important social institutions. These organizations and publications helped the immigrants both to adjust to their new lives and to keep alive the language and heritage of the Old Country.

Christian Rasmussen, often referred to as the "Danish Newspaper King" of the United States, published many newspapers, magazines, and books in Danish and other Scandinavian languages. This photo of his plant, located in Minneapolis, Minnesota, was taken in 1900.

The Danish Press in America

Because written Danish and Norwegian are almost identical, many early publications by Danes in the United States were cooperative ventures with Norwegians. Such was the case for *Skandinavia*, which made its appearance in New York City in 1847 and is credited with being the first newspaper published in the United States for Scandinavians. As time passed and the number of Danes in America increased, separate Danish and Norwegian publications began to appear. Although perhaps as many as 150 Danish-language periodicals were published at one time or another, most were short-lived. There was never a daily Danish paper, and a majority of the weeklies lasted a few years at most. Today only two Danish-language newspapers, *Den Danske Pioneer* and *Bien*, continue to be published in the United States.

Den Danske Pioneer (The Danish Pioneer) is the most successful paper in terms of circulation and long life. Founded in Omaha in 1872 by Mark Hansen, the *Pioneer* developed into a leading paper under the leadership of Sophus Neble, who purchased it in 1887. Circulation peaked in 1914 when the paper had 39,913 subscribers, mostly farmers in the Midwest.

Sophus Neble was fiercely democratic, and in his newspaper, he often attacked the Danish king and the nation's conservative government. Because of his critical editorials, the *Pioneer* was banned from Denmark for more than a decade. Despite his periodic unhappiness with the Danish government, Neble retained affection for the land of his birth and often used the pages of

This rare old photograph shows the staff of The Danish Pioneer *posing in front of the newspaper building in Omaha, Nebraska.*

BIEN

Since 1882

Thursday, October 16, 1986

Vejret i Danmark
i dag...13 gr. Celcius
(41/55 Fahrenheit—Klart)

ONLY DANISH WEEKLY NEWSPAPER PRINTED IN THE UNITED STATES

Thursday, October 16, 1986   Løssalgspris 40 cents   NUMBER 41

his paper to support relief projects for the poor on both sides of the Atlantic. By 1925, the Danish government had changed, and a new king made Neble a knight in recognition of his long career as a reporter and interpreter of Danish-American life.

After Neble's death in 1931, the paper was published by his wife. In 1958, it was moved from Omaha to Elmwood Park, a suburb of Chicago, where Hjalmer Bertelsen took over as publisher. Presently the *Pioneer* is edited and published biweekly by Chris Steffensen of Hoffman Estates, another Chicago suburb. Its circulation is about 4,000.

Bien (The Bee), the other surviving Danish-language paper, began in 1882 in San Francisco. Its circulation reached a peak of about 4,000 in the 1940s. Sophus Hartwick, the paper's most influential editor, believed that *Bien* should find its readership among the Danish communities on the West Coast. Since 1975, the weekly paper has been located in Los Angeles. The current publisher is Poul Dalby Andersen, and circulation is about 3,500.

Religious Organizations
Mormons, Baptists, Methodists, and Seventh-Day Adventists

As noted earlier, some Danish emigrants came to the United States for religious reasons, and, once settled in their new lives, maintained strong connections with their churches. Among these were Danish members of the Church of Jesus Christ of the Latter-day Saints, or Mormons. Although the Mormon church was not divided into distinct ethnic groups like the Lutheran and Catholic churches in the United States, Danes were so numerous in some areas of early Utah that they dominated local church life and frequently celebrated Danish holidays. From 1876 until 1935, there was a Danish-language Mormon weekly, *Bikuben (The Beehive)*.

47

Danish Baptists had also found a religious refuge in the United States. In 1864 a Danish-Norwegian Baptist Conference for the North-Western States was formed at Raymond, Wisconsin, near Racine. In 1910 the conference was divided along national lines, and the Danish Baptist Conference was established with perhaps 5,000 members. For a time the conference supported a seminary connected with Des Moines College, a Baptist school in Iowa. It also owned a Danish-language printing plant and published a hymnal.

The Methodist and Seventh Day Adventist churches also found adherents among Danish immigrants. In 1880 the Methodists created a Norwegian-Danish Conference, which remained in operation until 1943, when its members joined the English-speaking Methodist church. The number of Danish-American Methodists was small, perhaps 3,000 in 1910. Danish Seventh Day Adventists were even fewer, with only 800 or so of that faith in the same year.

Danish-American Lutherans

Since the vast majority of Danes who came to America were Lutheran, at least in name, the largest Danish-American religious organizations involved that church. Before 1870, Danes were too widely and thinly scattered to support separate Lutheran churches, so they often worshipped with Norwegian, Swedish, or German Lutherans. But as the number of Danes in the United States began to rise sharply after 1870, there was increased yearning among them for churches and pastors of their own.

At the same time, there was a gradual awakening in Denmark to the need for mission activities among Danes in the United States. Thus in 1869 there was formed in Denmark the Commission to Further the Preaching of the Gospel among Danes in North America. Although the commission was an independent and private body, it was recognized by the Danish government and received financial assistance from the state.

With aid from the commission, the Danish Evangelical Lutheran Church was formed in the United States in 1874. This church grew steadily, especially during the 1880s, the peak decade for Danish immigration. By 1890, it had 49 pastors at work in 89 parishes with a total membership of approximately 15,000.

Despite its promising beginnings, the Danish Evangelical Lutheran Church —usually referred to as the Danish Church—faced serious problems. The immigrants had brought deep religious divisions with them, and in the American climate of religious freedom, these became increasingly more difficult to bridge.

At the heart of the conflict were differing views over the Bible as the Word of God. One side was identified with the position of the famous 19th-century Danish bishop N. S. F. Grundtvig, who

A confirmation class at Bethlehem Lutheran Church in Askov, Minnesota, 1917. The church was an important part of community life in Askov as it was in most Danish immigrant settlements.

stressed the importance of the Apostle's Creed and the sacraments. These people, quite naturally, were called Grundtvigians.

Their opponents were called the Inner Mission. Stressing repentance and the development of a personal faith, Inner Mission preachers called upon converts to renounce such activities as drinking, dancing, gambling, and Sunday labor. Their pious practices and demands for a literal interpretation of the Bible put the Inner Mission in sharp contrast to the more worldly Grundtvigians.

Adding fuel to the smoldering fire was a dispute about assimilation. The Grundtvigians in the United States sought to keep as long as possible the Danish language and customs. The Inner Mission people, on the other hand, were more interested in becoming Americanized so that they could spread their religious message.

The differences within the Danish Church grew so serious that in 1892 it was forced to close its seminary at West Denmark, Wisconsin. Two years later the church was torn apart when the Inner Mission group departed to form its own organization. In 1896, those who

Bishop N. S. F. Grundtvig

language paper, *Kirkelig Samler*. In 1952, the group changed its name to the American Evangelical Lutheran Church, and in 1962 its 24,000 members joined with three groups of non-Danish Lutherans to form the Lutheran Church in America. In an effort to maintain some of their cultural identity after the merger, the Grundtvigians formed the Danish Interest Conference within the larger organization. This conference still publishes a semimonthly periodical, first called *Kirke og Folk* and now *Church and People*, and sponsors cultural and religious conferences.

The United Church, the other Danish Lutheran body, grew more rapidly; by 1950, it had 46,459 members, while the Danish Church had less than half that number. Most of the United Church pastors were trained at Trinity Seminary, Blair, Nebraska. Established in 1884 with one faculty member and four students, Trinity was the oldest Danish Lutheran Seminary in the United States. (In 1956 Trinity moved to the campus of Wartburg Seminary at Dubuque, Iowa, where four years later it was merged with that institution.)

Compared to its rival, the United Church more readily adopted the English language and, in 1944, dropped the word "Danish" from its official title. One clear indication of the language change is revealed by circulation statistics for its two major publications in 1959, the final year of publication. *Luthersk Ugeblad* had only 854 subscribers, while *The Ansgar Lutheran*, the English weekly, had over 12,000 subscribers.

had left the Danish Church joined with the Danish Evangelical Lutheran Church Association, an Inner Mission group that in 1884 had started a small church headquartered at Blair, Nebraska. This new body called itself the United Danish Evangelical Lutheran Church.

The Grundtvigian Danish Church, although weakened by the loss of one-third of its pastors and even more of its congregations, was soon able to build Grand View Seminary in Des Moines, Iowa. Until 1933, it published a Danish-

In 1960, the 60,000-member United Church merged with Norwegian and German churches to form the American Lutheran Church. A merger between the Lutheran Church in America and the American Lutheran Church is scheduled for 1988. After a century of division, the descendants of the Grundt-vigian and Inner Mission factions of Danish Lutheranism in the United States will be united.

Established in 1884, Trinity Seminary (left) trained ministers of the United Danish Evangelical Lutheran Church. Grand View Seminary (below) was associated with the Grundtvigian Danish Church. A merger in 1988 will finally unite these two branches of Danish Lutheranism.

This drawing shows the original folk-school building in Elk Horn, Iowa.

Education
The Folk School

One uniquely Danish contribution to American education is the folk school. The folk school was born in Denmark during the crisis of national spirit that followed the nation's disastrous alliance with France during the Napoleonic wars. Its father was N. F. S. Grundtvig, the theologian mentioned earlier.

Grundtvig sought some means of rousing his fellow Danes from their state of despair and finally stumbled on the idea of a school for young adults. (During this period, compulsory education in Denmark ended at age 14.) At Grundtvig's school, the emphasis was not to be on memory work or preparation for examinations but rather on discussions of life itself. There would be no entrance tests, final exams, or diplomas, just a comfortable atmosphere where young people could gather and learn as they chose.

By means of the folk school, Grundtvig and the other leaders of the movement hoped to increase their students' love of country and language. It was almost inevitable, therefore, that Danish emigrants to the United States, seeking to preserve their heritage, would turn to the folk school as a pattern for their first educational institutions.

The first Danish folk school in America was established at Elk Horn, Iowa, in 1878. Others soon followed: at Ashland, Michigan, in 1882; West Denmark, Wisconsin, in 1884; Nysted, Nebraska, 1887; Danebod at Tyler, Minnesota, in 1888; Atterdag at Solvang, California, in 1911; and Dalum in Alberta, Canada, in 1921. All of these schools were formed by leaders of the Grundtvigian faction of Danish-American Lutheranism. The only folk school with ties to the United Church was the Brorson Folk School at Kenmare, North Dakota, opened in 1905 by the celebrated lay preacher Jens Dixen.

Because most of these schools were founded and run by individual religious leaders, they often took on the character of their founder or current owner. Frequently students and faculty lived in the same building and took their meals together. The school curriculum included frequent lectures, but there was ample opportunity for group singing, gymnastics, and other activities.

A men's gymnastics group at the Danebod Folk School in Tyler, Minnesota, performs a routine in 1908.

For a time, the folk schools attracted immigrants and their children. In the long run, however, they could not overcome the problems of too few students —probably no more than 12,000 in combined attendance—and not enough money. By the time of World War I, the "golden age" of the Danish-American folk school had passed. Nysted, Danebod, Atterdag, and Dalum struggled into the 1930s, but the Depression finally forced them to close. The school buildings at Tyler were renovated in the 1940s and are still used for short-term conferences in the folk school tradition.

Higher Education

Today there are two liberal-arts colleges in the United States that grew out of educational institutions founded by Danish immigrants: Grand View College in Des Moines, Iowa, and Dana College, in Blair, Nebraska. Both originally shared campuses with theological seminaries and had as one of their main functions the preparation of students for formal religious training.

Opened in 1896, Grand View College was intended to serve as a theological seminary for the Danish Church following the split of 1894. From the beginning, however, the school offered non-theological courses. In 1912 an Academy Department, which gave high school credit, was added. Gradually the school began to stress college level work, and the academy was phased out. Grand View became an accredited jun-

ior college in 1938. Following the discontinuation of the seminary in 1959, it moved steadily toward becoming a four-year school and is now a college of the Lutheran Church in America.

The origins of Dana College are somewhat different. When Trinity Seminary opened at Blair in 1884, it also had a preparatory department for future seminary students. After the creation of the United Church in 1896, all preparatory work was moved to a school at Elk Horn, Iowa. For a variety of reasons, this separation of theological and preparatory work proved unsatisfactory. Thus in 1899 the leaders of the United Church voted to relocate all college-level classes to Blair.

The issue of what to call the seminary and its sister college was not resolved until 1903 when delegates to the United Church's annual convention decreed: "The name of the schools of the synod shall be Dana College and Trinity Seminary." (Dana is a poetic name for Denmark, and its use in that meaning was well known among many Danish Americans.)

Dana College granted its first Baccalaureate Degree in 1922. Following the departure of Trinity Seminary in 1956, there was a rapid expansion in student enrollment and physical facilities. In 1976, as part of the American Bicentennial celebration, Her Majesty Margrethe II, Queen of Denmark, visited the lovely hillside campus and gave the spring commencement address. Today Dana is a college of the American Lutheran Church.

Left: *Queen Margrethe II giving the commencement address at Dana College in 1976.* Below: *Balloons inscribed with Bible verses float over the campus of Dana, a college of the American Lutheran Church.*

A Fourth of July parade held in Racine, Wisconsin, during the early 1900s featured a float sponsored by the Dania Society.

Danish Fraternal Societies and Other Organizations

At one time or another, Danish Americans have formed well over 100 different organizations with as many as 500 local chapters or lodges. Just as had been the case with newspapers, some of the earliest Danish organizations were cooperative ventures with other Scandinavians. But in 1862, a society called Dania was created in Chicago to provide a variety of social and educational activities for the Danish immigrants. Eventually Dania's functions were broadened to include such things as health insurance, employment assistance, English lessons, and a missing-persons bureau. Dania and the Dania Ladies Society of Chicago continue to be active, though most of their work today involves hosting social functions.

Dania Societies were also formed in Racine, Wisconsin (1867), Oakland, California (1879), and Brooklyn, New York (1886). The Racine Dania has been a particularly active mutual aid and social society. In 1905, the present Dania Hall, a large brick structure built for the handsome sum of $35,000, was dedicated. Two women's groups were formed shortly thereafter, Dania's Daughters and Dania Ladies.

At the time of its centennial in 1979, Dania of California reported nearly 1,000 members in 17 local lodges in California and Nevada. The organization continues to stress its "modest benefit program" and a variety of social functions.

The largest nationwide Danish-American fraternal order is The Danish Brotherhood (originally *Det Danske Brodersamfund*). Founded in Omaha in 1882, the Brotherhood developed from several groups of Danes who were veterans either of the American Civil War or the Danish war with Prussia. From its beginnings, the Brotherhood has welcomed veterans and non-veterans alike, stressing that its membership was open to "honorable men, born of Danish parents or who were of Danish extraction."

Among the benefits offered by the Danish Brotherhood was life insurance for its members.

SUPREME LODGE OF DANISH BROTHERHOOD IN AMERICA.

Benefit Certificate of Danish Brotherhood
✕ ✕ IN AMERICA ✕ ✕

This Certifies That *Lars Petersen* has received the Degrees of MEMBERSHIP OF THE DANISH BROTHERHOOD IN AMERICA, and that he is a beneficiary member in good standing of Lodge No. *96* of said Order located at the City of *Jackson* in the State of *Minn* and that such person or persons as the said *Lars Petersen* may by will or by entry upon the records of the SUPREME LODGE of the DANISH BROTHERHOOD IN AMERICA, or upon the face of this Certificate name and nominate, will be entitled to receive from the DANISH BROTHERHOOD IN AMERICA, as a benefit at the death of said *Lars Petersen* such a sum of money not exceeding **FIVE HUNDRED DOLLARS,** as may be provided for by the constitution and by-laws of said Order, upon due notice and proof of death of the said *Lars Petersen* and upon the surrender of this Certificate, provided that the said *Lars Petersen* is in good standing as a member of said Order at the time of his death.

To the Officers of the Supreme Lodge of the Danish Brotherhood in America:

Brothers: I hereby nominate and name *my wife*

Marie Petersen

as the beneficiary of this Certificate and as the person to receive the money to be paid thereon.

Lars Petersen
Signature of Holder.

In Witness Whereof the said Danish Brotherhood in America has caused this instrument to be duly executed by its officers and attested by the seal of said Order this *21st* day of *April* 190 *5*

H. H. Vogt
SUPREME PRESIDENT.

J. Michaelsen
SUPREME SECRETARY.

The above Certificate delivered to the said *Lars Petersen*

in presence of

Danske Pioneer Trykkeri, Omaha.

The national headquarters of the Danish Brotherhood in America, located in Omaha, Nebraska, occupies a beautiful building that has won prizes for its architectural design.

Emphasizing social opportunities centered around a common Danish heritage and offering programs of life and health insurance, the Brotherhood grew rapidly. Within 10 years, it had 41 local lodges and nearly 2,000 members. The pattern of steady growth continued well into the 20th century, and by 1925, 21,000 people were members of the Danish Brotherhood in America.

When the Brotherhood celebrated its centennial in 1982, it reported having established 347 local lodges throughout the United States and Canada. There was even a lodge in Copenhagen for returned immigrants. Of this number, about 150 were still in operation. Today the Brotherhood publishes a monthly magazine, *The American Dane*, awards scholarships to children of members, and sponsors lectures on various aspects of Danish-American life. Even though the organization opened its membership to women in 1961, there remains a parallel group, the Danish Sisterhood, founded in Michigan in 1883.

Preserving the Danish Heritage in America

Over the years, Danes have formed several organizations or societies with the intent of preserving or interpreting their heritage. One of the earliest and most important of these was the Danish Folk Society, founded in 1887. In inviting others to join with them, the Folk Society's founders said: "It is our belief that the Danish people have a rich spiritual heritage..., and it is our hope that we Danes here in America will be able to contribute to making that heritage beneficial to others."

One of the leaders of the Folk Society was Frederik Lange Grundtvig, son of Bishop N. F. S. Grundtvig of Denmark. The younger Grundtvig had come to the United States originally to study birds but eventually became a pastor of a Danish Lutheran Church congregation in Clinton, Iowa. Grundtvig and others in the Folk Society tried to preserve their ethnic heritage by supporting the settlement of Danes in colonies throughout the United States and Canada. The best known of these communities are Askov, Minnesota; Danevang, Texas; Dagmar, Montana; and Solvang, California. Once the era of colony-founding passed, the Danish Folk Society gradually faded away.

In 1908, an urban organization, the Danish National Committee, was created in Chicago to increase cooperation among various Danish organizations in that city. Clubs, local lodges, and

Frederik Lange Grundtvig

churches were represented. A year after its founding, the committee started annual celebrations of Danish Constitution Day on June 5.

Eventually coordinating organizations similar to Chicago's DNC were created in other cities. In Minnesota's Twin Cities, for instance, the Danish-American Fellowship came into existence in 1948. Today several of these organizations continue to function, often sponsoring guest appearances by visiting Danish artists or scholars, hosting banquets and receptions for

Danish dignitaries, and, in the case of the Danish-American Fellowship, arranging charter flights to Denmark.

For a time after World War II, it appeared that the assimilation process would soon erase much of the Danish imprint from American life. But in the 1970s and 1980s, there was a revival of interest in the Danish-American experience, perhaps stimulated by the celebrations of the American Bicentennial and the great success of Alex Haley's *Roots*, the story of a black man's search for his own heritage.

In 1976, the Danish American Language Foundation was formed in Illinois to support *Den Danske Pioneer* and other publications in Danish. A year later, some people of Danish ancestry in Oregon took steps toward filling the long-felt need for a Danish-American historical association. Danes from across the United States and Canada responded enthusiastically, and the newly formed Danish American Heritage Society (DAHS) soon had over 500 dues-paying members. DAHS publishes a newsletter and a semiannual historical journal, *The Bridge*, which serves as an important outlet for scholarly research on Danish-American topics.

In addition, the DAHS has been very active in supporting two recent projects, the Danish Immigrant Archival Listing (DIAL) and the establishment of a Danish Immigrant Museum. DIAL is an attempt to prepare a listing of materials relevant to Danish-American history in more than 140 libraries and other institutions throughout the United States,

Thorvald Hansen, director of the Danish Immigrant Archival Listing, examines a document in the archives at Grand View College.

Canada, and Denmark. The director of the project is Thorvald Hansen, archivist for the Danish Immigrant Archives at Grand View College. Although the results of Hansen's efforts have yet to be published, they have inspired an interest in identifying and preserving valuable historical materials.

In 1980, Professor Norman C. Bansen of Dana College approached the DAHS with the suggestion that a museum be built somewhere in the United States to interpret Danish immigrant history. DAHS President Arnold Bodtker responded by appointing a committee headed by Dr. Signe Nielsen Betsinger to investigate the possibility of creating such a museum. After several meetings, the committee answered in the affirmative.

The next question was where should such an institution be located. Eventually two choices were presented: Minneapolis, Minnesota, or Elk Horn, Iowa. In February 1983, the committee met in Elk Horn. More than 500 local residents (including many from the nearby and equally Danish community of Kimballton) were in attendance, as were Iowa Governor Terry Branstad and several other state officials. Because of this tremendous display of enthusiasm and support, the committee voted to locate the museum in Elk Horn. The local Lutheran Church, one of the earliest formed by Danes in Iowa, gave the museum an attractive 20-acre site on the western edge of the community. In June 1983, the museum was incorporated and a Board of Directors

Dr. Signe Nielsen Betsinger is head of the committee making plans for the Danish Immigrant Museum to be established in Elk Horn, Iowa.

named. In September of the following year, June Stafford Sampson was named as the museum's director. Since then the Board of Directors has hired a professional consulting firm to plan a fund drive and has conferred with architects about designs for the museum building.

More than a century has passed since 1882, the peak year for the arrival of Danes in the United States. Today many descendants of those immigrants support institutions that are attempting to preserve or reclaim parts of the unique heritage of their Danish ancestry.

61

6
CONTRIBUTIONS TO AMERICAN LIFE

Gutzon Borglum, a sculptor of Danish ancestry, created the monumental carvings on Mount Rushmore.

Most Danes who emigrated to the United States were ordinary people seeking a better life for themselves and their children. Because they had much in common with the majority of the existing American population, many of them quickly blended into the American mainstream. So rapid, indeed, was the assimilation of Danish immigrants and their descendants that their contributions are often overlooked. Even so, it is possible to identify several Danes who have played a significant role in American life.

Agriculture

Agriculture is one area where Danes had impact. This is not surprising since so many of them were farmers who had learned important lessons from their experiences in Europe.

The cooperative creamery in Clarks Grove, Minnesota, was established in 1890.

By the 1880s, the peak decade for Danish emigration, a revolution was sweeping over rural Denmark. Cheap grain from Argentina, Russia, and the United States had driven the price of grain in northern Europe to such a low level that farmers found it difficult to make a profit. In a remarkably short span of time, Danish farmers shifted from raising grain for export to raising hogs, poultry, and milk cows for the production of bacon, eggs, and butter. One significant ingredient in this transformation was the establishment of producer cooperatives.

Immigrants brought information about these developments with them to the United States. Thus some of the earliest American agricultural cooperatives, especially in the area of dairying, were formed in Danish-American communities. The Clarks Grove Cooperative Creamery, for example, was one of the first and most successful of such ventures in Minnesota.

Throughout much of the Midwest, Danes frequently operated creameries and were considered excellent buttermakers. Two Danish residents of Fredsville, Iowa, Jeppe Slifsgaard and his son Truels, are credited with importing the first cream separator to the United

Niels Hansen was a pioneer horticulturalist who discovered many useful new varieties of plants.

his family emigrated to the United States. As a youth growing up in Des Moines, Iowa, Niels collected natural history specimens during long walks in the woods.

At the age of 17, Niels Hansen enrolled at Iowa State College. He received a degree in horticulture in 1887. After additional study and a period of work for commercial nurseries, Hansen secured a joint appointment on the faculty of South Dakota State College in Brookings and the staff of the Agricultural Experiment Station there.

Niels Hansen spent the next 40 years seeking and developing new varieties of grain, forage crops, and fruits that could withstand the cold, dry climate of the Northern Plains. As a pioneer "plant explorer," Hansen made several trips to Northern Europe and Asia in search of hardy plants. In 1897 he discovered a drought-resistant alfalfa in Turkestan and Siberia that could survive in the climate of the Dakotas and other Northern Plains states. On subsequent journeys, he not only brought back the seeds of an even hardier strain of alfalfa but also those for crested wheat grass, bromegrass, and the honeydew as well as other varieties of melons.

In addition to his plant introductions, Hansen's experiments in hybridization and selection made important contributions to improved varieties of apples, apricots, pears, and plums. Long before his death in 1950 at the age of 84, Niels Ebbesen Hansen was widely recognized as one of America's greatest horticulturalists.

States. It required two months, incidentally, for American customs officials in 1882 to decide how to tax the Danish-manufactured device for separating cream from milk. Because of their experience in dairy farming, some Danes eventually became professors of dairy husbandry at land grant colleges, while others served as state dairy commissioners or inspectors.

In contributions to American agriculture, few if any immigrants can match the achievements of Niels Ebbesen Hansen. Born on a Danish farm in 1866, Niels Hansen was seven when

The Arts
Painting, Sculpture, and Landscape Architecture

Christian Guldager, portrait painter of George Washington, is the best known of the early Danish-American artists, but several others have gained varying degrees of prominence. Carl Christian Anton Christensen, a Mormon who emigrated in 1857, created a remarkable series of paintings depicting several aspects of Mormon history, particularly the lengthy handcart trek to Salt Lake City. Peter Gui Clausen painted scenes of frontier life in Minnesota.

Two works by another Minnesota Dane, Ferdinand Reichardt, are part of the White House art collection. One painting of the upper Mississippi River by the Danish-born artist hangs in the China Room, where the presidential collection of porcelain is displayed.

This painting by Minnesota artist Ferdinand Reichardt, executed in 1857, pictures paddle-wheel steamboats on the upper Mississippi River.

The collections of many major museums include landscapes and seascapes by Emil Carlsen, who was born in 1853 and emigrated in 1872. More recently, some art critics have called Danish-born Olaf Wieghorst the "Dean of Western Painters." In 1983, one of Wieghorst's works, "Navajo Madonna," reportedly brought $450,000 from a private collector. President and Mrs. Reagan own four of his paintings. Not only has Wieghorst become a highly successful painter, but he has also appeared in two John Wayne films, playing the character of "Swede Larsen," an undertaker.

Two Danish-born sculptors who gained recognition in the late 19th century were Carl Rohl-Smith and Johanes Gelert. Among the most famous of Rohl-Smith's works are two sculptures that commemorate Civil War hero William Tecumseh Sherman and Iowa veterans of the Civil War.

Gelert is perhaps best remembered for his statue of a Chicago policeman, a tribute to the members of the police who were killed in that city's "Haymarket Riot" of 1886. This statue became a center of attention during the late 1960s when people unhappy with the behavior of the Chicago police attempted to destroy it. Eventually the statue was moved from Haymarket Square to a spot inside the police academy building. Less controversial is Gelert's statue of Hans Christian Andersen, which stands in Chicago's Lincoln Park. More than 10,000 attended its dedication in 1896.

By far the best known sculptor of Danish descent is Gutzon Borglum, the creator of the monumental "Shrine of Democracy" on the granite face of Mount Rushmore in the Black Hills of South Dakota. Borglum was born March 26, 1867, near Bear Lake in the Idaho Territory. His immigrant parents had taken the name Borglum from their home in Denmark. After he studied in San Francisco and Paris, some of his early works began to win prizes; in 1908 his marble bust of Lincoln was placed in the rotunda of the Capitol in Washington.

In 1915 Borglum was commissioned to create a gigantic memorial to the Confederacy at Stone Mountain, Georgia. Strong-willed and temperamental, Borglum would stand no criticism. In 1925, after a celebrated argument with leaders of the association organized to finance the memorial, he angrily smashed models for the sculpture and left Georgia with his work far from complete.

By this time, Borglum was already in contact with Doane Robinson, the State Historian of South Dakota. Robinson wanted the "hewer of mountains" to fashion some sort of monument in the Black Hills. After touring the area, Borglum chose Mt. Rushmore as the site for four giant busts of presidents Washington, Jefferson, Lincoln, and Theodore Roosevelt.

Work on the mountain began in 1927, and the project remained Borglum's chief preoccupation until his death in 1941. The small amount of unfinished work was completed by his son Lincoln,

The replica of Mount Rushmore in Denmark's Legoland (right) is an accurate copy of the majestic original carvings (above) in the Black Hills of South Dakota.

also a sculptor of considerable talent. The finished monument quickly became, and remains, one of America's major tourist attractions. For Danes and other Europeans who cannot make the journey to the Black Hills, a replica of Mt. Rushmore made from 1.5 million small plastic bricks now stands in Denmark's Legoland.

A portrait bust of landscape architect Jens Jensen sculpted by Christian Petersen, another Danish immigrant to the United States. Petersen was Artist-in-Residence at Iowa State College from 1934 to 1955.

One other Danish immigrant whose "artistry" on the landscape of America deserves mention is Jens Jensen. Born in 1860 in the area of South Jutland lost to Prussia four years later, Jensen came to America in 1884. The reason for his leaving had little to do with politics, however. Instead he was motivated by romance. The son of a wealthy landowner, he had fallen in love with the daughter of a poor family. When his own family forbade his marriage, Jensen sailed for the United States with his sweetheart. They were married after their arrival and settled in Chicago.

Jensen worked in the Chicago parks and eventually became superintendent and landscape architect of the entire West Chicago Park system. By 1920 he had earned an international reputation as a landscape artist and urban planner. Among his many achievements were the development of the first neighborhood park in any American city and the landscaping of Henry Ford's Dearborn estate. In 1935 Jens Jensen moved to Door County, Wisconsin, where he opened a school for landscape architects. He continued to teach until his death in 1951 at the age of 91.

Entertainment

Several Danes have gained national attention in various fields of entertainment. Jean Hersholt, for example, had a distinguished career as a movie actor and radio personality. Between 1914 and 1955, he appeared in more than 200 films. He played prominent roles in many classics of the silent screen, including *Greed, Stella Dallas,* and *The Mask of Fu Manchu.* In the 1930s, he created the immensely popular "Dr. Christian" radio character. In 1939 and 1941, he received special Academy Awards from the Academy of Motion Picture Arts and Sciences for his philanthropic efforts on behalf of his fellow actors.

Although he became an American citizen in 1918, Hersholt maintained close ties with the land of his birth. He accumulated the world's largest collection of Hans Christian Andersen letters, manuscripts, and first editions. Eventually Hersholt donated the Andersen material to the American Library of Congress "in gratitude for what this country has meant for me and my family."

Buddy Ebsen is another well-known actor of Danish descent. Best remembered for his starring roles in three long-running television shows—"Davy Crocket," "The Beverly Hillbillies," and "Barnaby Jones"—Ebsen started his career as a dancer. During the 1930s, he starred in Broadway shows and Hollywood musicals, often performing with his younger sister, Vilma. Ebsen has also

Above: *Jean Hersholt as the radio character Dr. Christian.* **Below:** *Buddy Ebsen*

Lauritz Melchior poses in front of a portrait showing the great tenor as Parsifal, a character from a Wagner opera. This photograph is part of the Melchior collection at Dana College.

appeared in many films and television dramas.

In the world of opera, few heroic tenors loomed larger, both literally and figuratively, than Lauritz Melchior. Born in Copenhagen in 1890, he attended the Royal Opera School and eventually became a great operatic tenor. He was a member of the Metropolitan Opera in New York from 1926 to 1950. Blessed with a voice of enormous range and strength, he won world-wide acclaim for his roles in the operas of Richard Wagner.

Following Melchior's death in 1973, some of the great singer's memorabilia, along with a large portion of his music library, was donated to Dana College, which created the "Lauritz Melchior Memorial Room" in its library to house the unique collection.

For the past 45 years, Americans of all ages of have enjoyed the performances of another Danish-born entertainer, the pianist and humorist Victor Borge. Borge fled Denmark after that country was occupied by the Germans early in World War II. The young refugee was virtually penniless and unable to speak or understand English when he arrived in the United States. By spending hours every day in movie theaters, Borge soon learned the language. A guest appearance on Bing Crosby's Kraft Music Hall radio program in 1941 was a great hit, and Borge's notable career was underway. He continues to be one of America's most popular concert performers, entertaining audiences with his unique combination of music and humor.

During a visit to Elk Horn, Iowa, popular entertainer Victor Borge talked to Lisa Riggs, owner of a gift shop at the Danish Windmill.

Peter Martins is yet another Dane with great talent who emigrated to the United States. In 1967, the 21-year-old Martins appeared as a guest artist with the New York City Ballet. Three years later, he became the company's principle dancer, and in 1983, he was appointed to the position of ballet master and co-director.

Martins is the best known of several Danish-trained stars who have dominated much of the dance world in recent decades. Others include Erik Bruhn, artistic director of the National Ballet of Canada from 1983 until his untimely death in 1986, the late Toni Lander of Ballet West in Salt Lake City, and Flemming Flindt of the Dallas Ballet.

Erik Bruhn, shown above in a performance with the Royal Danish Ballet, was one of the many outstanding Danish dancers who impressed North American audiences with their talent and style. Toni Lander (right) was a principle dancer with the American Ballet Theater and taught at Ballet West in Salt Lake City before her death in 1985.

Composer Libby Larsen (right) rehearses her choral symphony, Coming Forth into Day, *with Jehan el-Sadat (left), who collaborated in writing the text. Mrs. Sadat served as narrator when the work received its world premiere in 1986.*

The grandaughter of a Danish immigrant, Libby Larsen is an award-winning young composer whose works have been performed by orchestras throughout the United States. Ms. Larsen received her musical training at the University of Minnesota, where she studied with the well-known American composer Dominick Argento. In 1983, she was named Composer-in-Residence with the Minnesota Orchestra, and in 1985, her symphony *Water Music* was premiered by that orchestra under the baton of Sir Neville Marriner. Ms. Larsen's other compositions include a two-act romantic opera and a choral symphony, *Coming Forth into Day,* the text of which was written in collaboration with Jehan el-Sadat, the widow of Egypt's assassinated president.

Literature

The relatively small number of people in the world who read Danish greatly limits the potential market for authors who write in that language. Nevertheless, even among the much smaller Danish-American population, several such writers were able to find readers for their works. The most successful writers in Danish were Adam Dan, Kristian Østergaard, Carl Hansen, and the poet Anton Kvist. A later immigrant, Enok Mortensen, was bilingual and wrote novels, short stories, and historical studies in both Danish and English.

An outstanding Danish-American writer who wrote in English was Sophus Kieth Winther. Born in Denmark in 1893, he was only two when his parents emigrated to the United States. Winther grew up on a farm near Weeping Water, Nebraska, but at the age 18, he and his parents moved to Oregon. In 1927 he received a Doctor of Philosophy degree from the University of Washington and remained there as a member of the English faculty until his retirement in 1963.

Among Winther's many published works are a critical study of the American author Eugene O'Neill and several novels, among them *Beyond the Garden Gate* and the Grimsen trilogy: *Take All To Nebraska*, 1936; *Mortgage Your Heart*, 1937; and *This Passion Never Dies*, 1938. The trilogy portrays the hard life of the fictional Grimsen family, Danish immigrant farmers in Nebraska.

More recently, Julie Jensen McDonald

Sophus Kieth Winther as a young man

has written several books about Iowa Danes. In *Amalie's Story* (1970), a highly acclaimed novel, she describes the difficulties experienced by Danish immigrants in adapting to a new land.

Politics

The "ordinary" people who made up the bulk of Danish emigration to the United States had obtained the political

74

Frederick Valdemar Peterson (right), shown here with fellow Republican Richard M. Nixon, was governor of Nebraska from 1947 to 1953. Later in his career, he served as U. S. ambassador to both Denmark and Finland.

rights of voting and office holding before departing Denmark. They eagerly sought these same rights in their new homeland. Danes were quick to become citizens and participate in American elections. But because they were so small in number and so widely scattered, they were seldom able to form effective voting blocs. Except for local races in certain counties in western Iowa and eastern Nebraska, Danish-American politicians seeking state or national offices had to find support among non-Danes.

Despite this, politicians of Danish ancestry have served as governors of several states, including Minnesota, Nebraska, and California. Danes and their descendants have also been elected to the United States Congress.

Ben Jensen represented Iowa's Seventh District in the House of Representatives for 13 terms between 1938 and 1964. The 10th of 13 children born to an emigrant ditch digger and his wife, Jensen was christened "Ben the Tenth." When this caused him trouble in school, he announced that his name was Benton (after an Iowa county) Franklin (after Benjamin Franklin) Jensen. During World War II, Jensen assisted the Office of War Information in the preparation of Danish-language shortwave broadcast to German-occupied Denmark. In 1954 he was one of five Congressmen wounded when Puerto Rican extremists opened fire on the House of Representatives. Jensen even-

tually became the ranking Republican on the powerful House Appropriations Committee.

Lloyd Bentsen, Jr., has represented Texas in the Senate since 1971. Previously he served three terms in the House. Senator Bentsen's grandfather, Peter Bentsen, was 19 when he emigrated to the United States in 1884. He soon settled in South Dakota, where he married Tena Petersen five years later. After years of hard struggle, the Bentsens became successful farmers. In 1918 they moved to the Rio Grande Valley of Texas, in part to escape the harsh Dakota winters. At the end of World War I, their two sons, Lloyd and Elmer, began buying low-priced south Texas

Two Danish-American members of the United States Congress: Ben Jensen (left) and Lloyd Bentsen (right)

land. Once planted with citrus orchards or other crops, the land rose sharply in value. By the end of World War II, the Bentsen brothers controlled 100,000 acres and had become prominent Texas businessmen and ranchers. Lloyd, Jr., carried on the family tradition by becoming a successful businessman before entering politics. By 1980 there were 114 Bentsen family descendants, many of them notable in a wide variety of businesses or professions—a true "Texas dynasty."

The son of Danish immigrants, Ancher Nelsen represented Minnesota's Second Congressional District in the United States House of Representatives from 1958 to 1974. Earlier in his career, he served as administrator of the National Rural Electrification program, which brought electricity to many farm regions of the country. When King Frederik IX of Denmark died in 1972, Nelsen was one of those chosen to represent the United States at the funeral. Later, he wrote about his official visit to the homeland of his immigrant parents:

Ancher Nelsen, the son of Danish immigrants, represented the United States at the funeral of King Frederick IX.

Nels Peter Nielsen and his bride, the former Elisabeth Anderson, looked to the United States as a new home. Both about 24, they booked passage from Denmark on the cheapest line at the lowest rate available. . . . They arrived in America with little in their pockets but much in their hearts, including pride, determination and a deeply religious conviction and dedication. . . . Theirs was the legacy and tradition that has helped to build America. It was my great honor to bear this legacy with me from this great land of opportunity in returning to their homeland for the burial of a king.

Strangely, the Dane who had the greatest impact upon American political life never held elective office. His name was Jacob August Riis. Born May 3, 1849, in Ribe, one of Denmark's oldest cities, Jacob was the son of a school teacher and part-time newspaper publisher. Although his father urged Jacob to choose one of these occupations, the boy decided on carpentry and, after four years service as an apprentice, received his journeyman's certificate. By this time, however, he had fallen in love with the daughter of a rich manufacturer. When her family rejected him as a suitor, a broken-hearted, 21-year-old Jacob Riis emigrated to America. (Unlike many similar stories, this one has a happy ending. Some years later Jacob learned that his childhood sweetheart was still single, and during a return visit to Ribe, they were married.)

In common with the experience of many other immigrants, Riis' first years in the United States were filled with hardships and a variety of laboring jobs. Eventually the young Dane landed a position as a newspaper reporter, and journalism became his career. First for the *New York Tribune* and then the *Evening Sun*, Riis wrote about the poverty and abuse suffered by the poor who were crowded into the tenements of the nation's largest city.

To aid in his exposes on the miserable lives of many New Yorkers, Riis learned to use a camera and became America's first journalist-photographer. He pioneered the use of flash and was thus able to photograph the interiors of slum

dwellings. His book, *How the Other Half Lives* (1890), was the first description of social conditions within the inner city to be accompanied by photographs. The book was a sensation and went through many editions.

Shortly after *How the Other Half Lives* first appeared, Theodore Roosevelt visited the Riis home and left a card with the message: "I have read your book and have come to help." The two men soon became great friends, and on several occasions, as governor of New York and later as president, Roosevelt offered Riis appointment to high office. But Riis always declined, saying that he was too busy to enter politics.

Jacob Riis continued to write and lecture about the need for reform, including child labor laws, better sanitation, and more neighborhood parks and school playgrounds. Long before his death in 1914, he had become one of America's most famous immigrants. His autobiography, *The Making of an American* (1901), was a best seller, and Theodore Roosevelt frequently quoted with approval a description of Riis as "New York's most useful citizen."

78

A 1903 photograph of Jacob A. Riis, "New York's most useful citizen" and one of the world's foremost photo journalists

Business and Manufacturing

The records of American history contain many accounts of poor immigrants who found success in America. Some of those for whom the United States was a land of opportunity were Danes. Niels Poulsen (anglicized to Poulson after he came to America) was the son of a Danish day laborer. After spending his childhood years stripping tobacco leaves, he was apprenticed as a mason when he was 14. Poulson studied mechanical theory and drawing in night school, and at the age of 21, he left for the United States.

He worked in New York first as a bricklayer and later as an architectural draftsman. Then in 1876 he joined with Charles M. Eiger to create the firm eventually known as the Hecla Architectural Iron Works. With the help of more than 1,000 employees, some of them artists and metallurgists, Poulson and his partner designed and produced remarkable structural and ornamental details in iron. Their creations were used in the construction of some major New York buildings, among them the Grand Central and Pennsylvania railroad stations. Poulson's own "ironhouse," a personal home constructed almost entirely of steel and copper, was a showplace in Brooklyn until it was leveled in 1930.

In 1910, Poulson gave $100,000 to the newly formed American Scandinavian Foundation. A year later, shortly before

This portrait of Niels Poulson by Danish artist Thomas Martin Jensen hangs in the offices of the American Scandinavian Foundation in New York City.

his death, he made an additional gift of $500,000. Poulson's "noble gesture" ensured the survival and growth of the ASF—"the very first private organization in the United States formed for the sole purpose of advancing cultural and educational exchange between the United States and a group of other countries."

Another Dane whose work with metals made a significant contribution to American life was William Petersen, the creator of the famous VISE-GRIP locking wrench. Trained as a blacksmith,

William Petersen and his famous invention

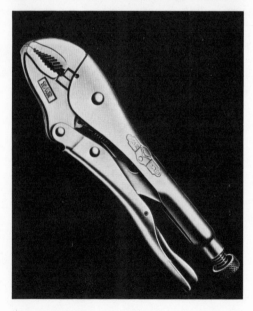

Petersen was 21 when he came to the United States in 1901. "Smithies" were in great demand in farming areas, and he soon was plying his trade in the small town of DeWitt, Nebraska.

With the development of the automobile, however, agriculture and transportation moved away from dependence on animal power, and there was a declining need for horseshoeing, which was a significant part of the blacksmith's work. With time on his hands, Petersen began to experiment and invent. In 1921, he patented a wrench with a vise-like grip. Three years later, he improved the design by adding a locking lever. As a trademark for his invention, he registered the name VISE-GRIP.

Manufacturing problems limited sales until 1934 when Petersen and his four children, Ralph, Christian, Richard, and Harriet, formed the Petersen Manufacturing Company in DeWitt. Each member of the family contributed to the expansion of the company, and sales began to increase. Several new tools were designed and developed, and in 1969, the company opened an international office in Chicago. By the early 1980s, more than 600 workers in DeWitt were turning out between 40,000 and 50,000 tools per day—an extraordinary legacy from a immigrant blacksmith who had both an idea and the determination to make it work.

Lorenz Iversen was another Dane who rose to great heights in the world of American business. Educated as a mechanical engineer at a German university, Iversen came to the United

States in 1902 and went to work as a draftsman at the Mesta Machine Company near Pittsburgh. He moved rapidly upward through company ranks and became its president in 1930, a position he would hold until his retirement in 1963 at the age of 87.

Under Iversen's leadership, Mesta became one of the world's largest manufacturers of heavy machinery. Today there are over 500 steel mills around the world using Mesta machinery. During World War II, Mesta foundries and machine shops produced the famous "Long-Tom" artillery pieces, 155-mm cannons capable of delivering 100 pound shells with devastating accuracy upon targets 15 miles away, as well as scores of other weapons that helped to make the United States the "arsenal of democracy." The gigantic Mesta plant in Homestead, Pennsylvania, became so famous that it was toured by world leaders such as President Franklin D. Roosevelt and Soviet Premier Nikita Khrushchev.

Although nearly 20 years have passed since Lorenz Iversen's death, many retired Mesta workers remember the Danish immigrant whom they called "Pappy" with a great deal of affection. "He was the Mesta Machine Company," said one former shop foreman in a 1984 story about Iversen in the *Wall Street Journal*.

The contributions of the Mesta Manufacturing Company to American efforts in World War II were significant, but they were overshadowed by those of another Dane, William S. Knudsen,

William S. Knudsen

who directed much of the nation's wartime production. Born in Copenhagen in 1879 and christened Signius Wilhelm Poul, young Wilhelm was a good student with an interest in mechanical design. Immigrating to the United States in 1900, he reportedly arrived in New York with $30 in his pocket.

When the timekeeper on the young Dane's first job complained about recording his lengthy name, he became "William S. Knudsen." Because he stood six feet, three inches tall and weighed 235 pounds, most people, however, simply called him "Big Bill." Many years later, a writer for *Fortune* magazine said being close to Knudsen was "like being in the room with a well-dressed

An early assembly line at a Ford plant. Danish immigrant William Knudsen supervised the mass production techniques that supplied the parts for this new and efficient manufacturing system.

and highly intelligent polar bear who speaks with a low, liquid accent."

After brief stints at a shipyard and a railroad shop, Knudsen became a mechanic in the J. R. Kiem Mills, a bicycle parts factory. In 1911, auto king Henry Ford bought the factory, which had been converted to the manufacture of auto parts. Knudsen, by now assistant superintendent, went to work for Ford. Soon the husky Dane was supervising the complex techniques of mass production in the 27 Ford assembly plants.

During World War I he was head of production for the legendary Model T.

After leaving Ford in 1921, William Knudsen became president of the Chevrolet Division of General Motors. Under his brilliant leadership, Chevrolet soon challenged Ford for auto sales supremacy. In 1937 Kundsen became president of General Motors, then the largest manufacturing corporation in the world. With salary and bonuses frequently topping half a million dollars annually, Kundsen was one of America's 10 highest paid individuals during the 1930s.

When President Franklin D. Roosevelt called upon "Big Bill" to guide the development of a defense production program at the beginning of World War II, Knudsen insisted that his government salary be a token one dollar per year. In recognition of his important positon, Knudsen finally accepted an army commission as a lieutenant general in 1942 (the only civilian in American history appointed directly to that high rank). He continued to supervise a variety of production operations, by one count visiting 1,200 factories as chief of some 11 million war workers. He left military service at the end of the war and died in 1947 at the age of 67, truly a giant among the architects of the modern industrial economy.

William S. Knudsen's son, Semon Emil, or "Bunkie," as everyone called him, was also a highly successful automotive executive. Bunkie Knudsen went to work with General Motors as an engineer in 1939. Following the war, he supervised installation of automated tools on GM's assembly lines. In 1956 he was named head of the company's Pontiac Division. Four years later he became president of Chevrolet. When passed over for the presidency of General Motors in 1968, Knudsen resigned. A week later he was appointed president of the Ford Motor Company, the auto firm his illustrious father had done so much to build. From 1971 to 1979, he was chairman of the board of directors and chief executive officer of the White Motor Corporation.

Max Henius

Science and Technology

Although fewer Danes were attracted to science and technology than to industry, some names stand out. Max Henius, born in Aalborg, Denmark, in 1859, was a chemist of great importance in the American fermentation industry. Five years after he emigrated to America in 1886, Henius joined with Robert Wahl to form the company of Wahl & Henius, analytical and consulting chemists. Out of this firm evolved the Wahl-Henius Institute, which served brewers all over the world.

Henius' skills as a chemist were crucial in his successful effort to pinpoint the source of a typhus epidemic that threatened Chicago in 1892. After much investigation, he finally traced the source of the disease to milk that had been diluted with polluted water from Lake Michigan. Henius was also the prime mover in the creation of Denmark's Rebild National Park where the independence of the United States is celebrated every Fourth of July.

And what would Fourth of July celebrations be without speeches? Public speaking on any occasion became considerably easier with the development of the loudspeaker by Danish-born Peter Jensen and his American partner, Edwin S. Pridham. The two men successfully demonstrated their dynamic horn loudspeaker, which they called "Magnavox" (Great Voice), at a football game in San Francisco in 1915. Jensen and Pridham continued to refine their invention and, in September 1919, received their greatest recognition when President Woodrow Wilson addressed a crowd of approximately 50,000 people at a San Diego stadium over a sound system using two Magnavox speakers.

In the mid 1920s, Jensen left Magnavox to found the Jensen Radio Manufacturing Company. Later he also created Jensen Industries to produce phonograph needles. During World War II, he was a government consultant in the areas of radio and radar. His contributions to American life were summarized in an obituary in the *Journal of Audio Engineering Society* (January 1962): "... of the many men who distinguished themselves in the early years of audio engineering, Peter Jensen was undoubtedly one of the most creative and productive. His inventions, experiments and sound systems were the heralds of today's high fidelity industry."

Education

Most Danish immigrants were firm believers in the value of education, and they supported both public education and a wide variety of private educational institutions in the United States. In addition, Danish Americans have had distinguished careers in several fields of education.

The theologian-historian Peder Sørensen Vig was the most important early recorder of Danish-American history. President of Trinity Seminary in Blair, Nebraska, from 1897 to 1926 with the exception of two brief periods, Vig was a prolific writer. He produced 10 books and 8 shorter works about Danes in the United States. His *Danske i Amerika* (1907) remains the most valuable source of information on Danish immigrants in the United States.

Unlike Vig, whose interest was narrowly focused on Danes, Marcus Lee Hansen was a historian of all American immigrants. The son of a Danish-born father and a Norwegian-born mother, Hansen earned bachelor's and master's degrees at the University of Iowa in 1916 and 1917. He obtained his Ph.D. in history at Harvard, where he studied under Frederick Jackson Turner, one of America's renowned historians.

The most significant years of Hansen's academic career were spent at the University of Illinois. He also devoted a great deal of his life to research in European and American archives, seeking information about the migration of peoples across the Atlantic. In 1941, three years after his death from kidney disease at the age of 46, his scholarly efforts were honored when his book, *The Atlantic Migration*, was awarded the Pulitzer Prize for history. Today Hansen is acclaimed as the pioneering scholar on the influence of immigration upon the American character.

Another educator of Danish descent who had an impact upon American life was the economist Alvin Harvey Hansen. Born in Viborg (named after a city in Denmark), South Dakota, in 1887, Hansen attended Yankton College and the University of Wisconsin. He taught at the universities of Wisconsin, Minnesota, and Brown before joining the Harvard faculty in 1937.

A follower of the economic theories of John Maynard Keynes, Hansen had enormous influence in shaping government policies from the 1930s until well into the 1950s. He helped to create the Social Security System in 1935 and, at the end of World War II, assisted in drafting the Full Employment Act of 1946, which established the Council of Economic Advisors. Hansen wrote or co-authored 15 books, including *The American Economy*, which was widely read. Upon his retirement from Harvard in 1956, he lectured at many institutions, including the University of

Marcus Lee Hansen received the Pulitzer Prize for one of his scholarly books on immigration to North America.

Bombay, Yale, and Michigan State.

From early Danish explorers to plain farm folk seeking land of their own to entertainers desiring a larger audience, Danes have been a part of American life. Some became famous; most did not. But both the famous and the not-so-famous have left their imprint. In spite of their comparatively small numbers, Danish immigrants have enriched the history of America.

Alvin Harvey Hansen was an influential economist whose ideas helped to shape U. S. government policy.

Peder Hansen (left) emigrated to the United States in 1882 at the age of 14 and eventually became a successful farmer in the Midwest. In this photo, Peder, his wife, Anna, and their son, Harold, are shown posing proudly with some of their farm animals.

The four Christiansen brothers—Rasmus, Peder, Hans, and Anders—made new lives in the United States after emigrating from Denmark during the late 1800s and early 1900s. Among their many American descendants is Anna Larsen (below right), shown here in 1910 at the age of 12. Anna still lives in Jackson County, Minnesota, where her Danish ancestors first settled.

The son of Danish immigrants, Gutzon Borglum created an enduring monument to the American spirit at Mount Rushmore.

INDEX

Clausen, Claus L., 35
Clausen, Peter Gui, 65
Commission to Further the Preaching of
  the Gospel among Danes in North America, 48
cooperatives, agricultural, 63
Copenhagen, 10
Council Bluffs, Iowa, 42

Dagmar, Montana, 59
dairying, 63-64
Dan, Adam, 74
Dana College, 54-55
Danebod, 53, 54
Danevang, Texas, 59
Dania Societies, 56-57
Danish-American Fellowship, 59, 60
Danish American Heritage Society, 60, 61
Danish Baptist Conference, 48
Danish Brotherhood, The, 57-58
Danish Evangelical Lutheran Church
  (Danish Church), 37, 48-50, 54
Danish Evangelical Lutheran Church
  Association, 50
Danish Folk Society, 38, 41, 59
Danish Immigrant Archival Listing, 60-61
Danish Immigrant Museum, 60, 61
Danish Interest Conference, 50
Danish National Committee, 59
Danish-Norwegian Baptist Conference for
  the North-Western States, 48
Danish Sisterhood, 58
Danish West Indies Company, 16
Dannebrog (Danish flag), 7, 39
Danske i Amerika, 86
*Danske Pioneer, Den (The Danish
  Pioneer),* 45-47, 60
Denmark: economy of, 9-10, 29-31, 63;
  history of, 12-13, 26, 27-28;
  population of, 8, 29-30; tourism in, 10-11
Dixen, Jens, 53

Ebsen, Buddy, 69-70
Elk Horn, Iowa, 36, 61; folk school at, 53

Febiger, Hans Christian, 18-19

Flight to America, The, 31
folk schools, 52-54
Fredsville, Iowa, 35
Fribert, Laurits Jacob, 33

Geleff, Poul, 26-27
Gelert, Johanes, 66
Grand View College, 54
Grand View Seminary, 50, 54
Grattinger, Iowa, 35
Grundtvig, Frederik Lange, 59
Grundtvig, N. S. F., 48-49, 52
Grundtvigians, 49, 50, 53
Guldager, Christian, 19, 65

Hansen, Alvin Harvey, 87
Hansen, Carl, 74
Hansen, Marcus Lee, 86-87
Hansen, Mark, 46
Hansen, Niels Ebbesen, 64
Hansen, Peter O. and Hans Christian, 24
Hansen, Thorvald, 61
Hartwick, Sophus, 47
Henius, Max, 85-86
Hersholt, Jean, 69
Homestead Act, 35
Hvidt, Kristian, 30

Inner Mission, 49-50
Iowa, Danish settlements in, 23, 35-36
Iversen, Lorenz, 82-83

Jansen family (Danish settlers in New
  Netherlands), 17
Jensen, Ben, 76
Jensen, Jens, 68
Jensen, Peter, 86

Kansas, Danish settlements in, 27
Kirkelig Samler, 50
Kirke og Folk (Church and People), 50
Knudsen, Semon Emil (Bunkie), 85
Knudsen, William S. 83-85
Købner, Julius, 23
Kuyter, Jochem Pietersen, 17
Kvist, Anton, 74

91

Vikings, 12

Wartburg Seminary, 50
Washington, George, 18, 19
Washington state, Danish settlements in, 41
Werner, Christian, 18
Wieghorst, Olaf, 66
Winther, Christian, 31
Winther, Sophus Kieth, 74
Wisconsin, Danish settlements in, 23, 34, 35

Young, Brigham, 24

Zanco, Charles, 19

ACKNOWLEDGMENTS The photographs in this book are reproduced through the courtesy of: pp. 1, 43, 57, 88 (bottom), 89 (top and lower right), Elizabeth M. Petersen; pp. 6, 7, 9, 10, 11 (bottom), 13 (bottom), 30, 72 (left), Danish Tourist Board; p. 11 (top), 67 (bottom), Shirley Petersen; p. 12, Viking Ship Museum, Roskilde, Denmark; p. 13 (top), Mansell Collection; pp. 14, 21, Lassen Volcanic National Park; p. 15, Hakluyt Society; p. 16, U. S. Virgin Islands; p. 18, The J. Clarence Davies Collection, Museum of the City of New York; p. 19, Massachusetts Historical Society; pp. 20 (top), 70, Institute of Texan Cultures at San Antonio; pp. 20 (bottom), 34, 83, Library of Congress; pp. 22, 32, 45, 85, Det Danske Udvandrerarkiv; p. 24, Independent Picture Service; p. 25, Utah State Historical Society; pp. 26, 27, Arbejderbevaegelsens Arkiv og Bibliotek; p. 29, Peter L. Petersen; p. 33, Aarhus Art Museum; p. 35, State Historical Society of Wisconsin; pp. 37, 63, 65, Minnesota State Historical Society; p. 38, Pine County Historical Society; p. 39, Josephine Krogh; p. 40, Verner A. Petersen, Danevang, Texas, photo courtesy Institute of Texan Cultures at San Antonio; p. 41, Santa Ynez Valley Visitors Bureau; p. 44, Lisa Riggs; p. 46, *Den Danske Pioneer;* p. 47, *Bien;* p. 49, Rosie Christensen; pp. 50, 51 (bottom), 53, 59, 60, 96, Thorvald Hansen, Danish Immigrant Archives; pp. 51 (top), 52, 55, 70 (Lauritz Melchior Room), 94, Dana College; p. 56, Dania Society, Racine, Wisconsin; p. 58, Danish Brotherhood in America; p. 61, Signe Nielsen Betsinger; pp. 62, 67 (top), 89 (bottom left), Mount Rushmore National Memorial; p. 64, *American Review of Reviews;* p. 68, Iowa State University Press, photograph by Connie Svoboda; p. 69, Collectors Bookstore; p. 71, Earl Sampson; p. 72 (right), Ballet West; p. 73, Libby Larsen; p. 74, Special Collections Division, University of Washington Libraries; p. 75, Nebraska State Historical Society; p. 76 (left), Special Collections, University of Iowa; p. 76 (right), Senator Lloyd Bentsen; p. 77, Former Congressman Ancher Nelsen; pp. 79, 80, Museum of the City of New York; p. 81, American Scandinavian Foundation; p. 82, Petersen Manufacturing Company; p. 84, Ford Motor Company; p. 87, University of Illinois; p. 88 (top), Harvard University Archives. Front cover photograph: Peter L. Petersen. Back cover photographs: Petersen Manufacturing Company (upper left); Mount Rushmore National Memorial (lower left); Elizabeth M. Petersen (right).

PETER L. PETERSEN is a historian with a long-standing interest in the ethnic heritage of the American people, especially the Scandinavian experience in the United States. The grandson of Danish immigrants who settled in western Iowa, Dr. Petersen is the author of many publications on American immigration, including studies of Norwegian settlers in Texas and Danes in Iowa. He has also written a history of Trinity Seminary and Dana College, institutions important in the history of Danish life in the United States. Active in Danish-American organizations, Dr. Petersen currently serves on the Board of Directors for the Danish Immigrant Museum, Elk Horn, Iowa, and on the editorial board of *The Bridge*, the journal of the Danish-American Heritage Society.

Peter L. Petersen holds degrees in history from Dana College, the University of South Dakota, and the University of Iowa. He is a member of the history department at West Texas State University, where students have twice selected him as "outstanding member of the faculty." Dr. Petersen lives in Canyon, Texas, with his wife, Shirley, and their two sons.

THE *IN AMERICA* SERIES

AMERICAN IMMIGRATION
THE **AMERICAN INDIAN,** VOL. I
THE **AMERICAN INDIAN,** VOL. II
THE **ARMENIANS**
THE **BLACKS**
THE **CHINESE**
THE **CZECHS & SLOVAKS**
THE **DANES**
THE **DUTCH**
THE **EAST INDIANS & PAKISTANIS**
THE **ENGLISH**
THE **FILIPINOS**
THE **FINNS**
THE **FRENCH**
THE **GERMANS**
THE **GREEKS**
THE **HUNGARIANS**

THE **IRISH**
THE **ITALIANS**
THE **JAPANESE**
THE **JEWS**
THE **KOREANS**
THE **LEBANESE**
THE **MEXICANS**
THE **NORWEGIANS**
THE **POLES**
THE **PUERTO RICANS**
THE **RUSSIANS**
THE **SCOTS & SCOTCH-IRISH**
THE **SWEDES**
THE **UKRANIANS**
THE **VIETNAMESE**
THE **YUGOSLAVS**

Lerner Publications Company
241 First Avenue North · Minneapolis, Minnesota 55401